# 6 Weeks to Sales Confidence: A Guide for Women

By Jula Pereira

# Dedication

For my mom, my sister, and all the powerful women in my life.

# Table of Contents

Day 12: Creating a Sales Scripts

Day 13: Building Rapport

Day 14: Framing the Call

Day 15: Asking Guiding Questions

**Week 4**

Day 16: Reviewing the Budget

Day 17: Transitioning to Your Offer

Day 18: Pitching and Asking for the Sale

Day 19: Answering Questions / Overcoming Objections

Day 20: Reviewing Next Steps with the Prospective Client

**Week 5**

Day 21: Practicing Your Script

Day 22: Recording Your Calls

Day 23: Note Taking and Tracking Your Clients

Day 24: Following Up

Day 25: Mindset Routine for Sales

**Week 6**

Day 26: Developing a Resilient Mind

**Conclusion: Learning to Trust Yourself**

# Introduction

Does the idea of sales terrify you? Welcome to the club! As a woman entrepreneur who's passionate about her mission, it can often feel quite intimidating to get on the phone with someone and actually have to share a price for your services. Why can't we all barter our services with each other?

You actually have more strength, skills, and aptitude to learn than you give yourself credit for. Contrary to what many people think, sales can be learned. It is not a skill or talent that you're born with. Being able to sell yourself is revealed in many different ways. Selling is essentially learning to influence another person, and that ability is a coveted skill.

Imagine what your life would be like if you were more easily able to impact another person. Yes, there are people out there who influence others in bad ways, but persuasion can also happen in a good way. If you have kids, you are nudging them on a daily basis
in a positive direction because you care deeply about their growth and development.

That motivation is the same with your prospective client. You care so much about them that you are excited to help them on their journey. It is your mission to share that enthusiasm with your clients.

As a social media strategist and sales for coach for women, I've worked with hundreds of people who were really afraid of putting themselves out in the world. So many of my clients were incredible at what they did, but they often had a hard time articulating that passion to other people.

Being exposed on social media and sales calls left them feeling intimidated by the whole process of trying to sell. They also had a hard time celebrating their wins and learning how to bring these achievements out in their sales process without feeling like they were bragging about their accomplishments.

I decided to focus this book specifically for women entrepreneurs for a few reasons, because I saw a lot of women (myself included!) who downplayed their own greatness and had a hard time asserting themselves in the sales process.

I know this feeling on a very deep, visceral level because I experienced it much of my own life. Growing up, I didn't have a lot of confidence and had a hard time standing up for myself when I was bullied in middle school and junior high. I am East-Indian ethnically, but when I was young, I wanted to be white. I did not believe in myself, even though I had a few prominent figures in my life who did believe in my abilities.

After graduating college with a degree in Comparative Literature, I was absolutely clueless about what I wanted to do with my life. I embarked on a stream of random, unsatisfying jobs, such as working at a group home for emotionally-disturbed teenage girls, being a typist at a newspaper, doing massage therapy and holistic lifestyle consulting, and finally working at a non-profit for seven years, earning $20 per hour.

When my non-profit job relocated and I was unable to find a full-time position in marketing, I decided to start my own social media marketing business with the encouragement of my partner and some close friends. That decision changed everything for me. For the first time, I utilized my skills to connect with people and my business grew, to a point.

But I still struggled with breaking through my own glass ceiling. I paid $10k for an online coaching program because I didn't have the confidence to truly bring myself out to the world, and I thought I needed someone else to guide me. I crashed in the summer of 2018, and had to reassess my life and my business. I was stressed about money all the time and I didn't have a solid foundation for my growth.

That's when my perspective changed dramatically. Broke and in $22,000 in debt, I got a job at a digital marketing agency and volunteered to do business development for them. Through that position, I learned that I particularly excelled in sales and that implementation was not right for me. Over the next four months, I was able to pay back my entire debt. I turned my life around with the support of my partner and also going to therapy.

Through therapy, I dealt with some difficult, deep-seated feelings from the past, and I was able to finally ignite my inner passion and drive. I realized that if I could help other women entrepreneurs alleviate their fear and anxiety around sales, gain the confidence to price themselves right, and onboard new clients more easily, I could help them have a greater impact in general. And that influence would ripple out to the world.

Just like me, many women entrepreneurs genuinely want to make an impact, but they have a very difficult time knowing what to charge to reflect the value they bring, or they experience challenges selling their services. They often struggle with their own money beliefs or have a hard time transitioning from helping a prospective client to asking for the sale.

I personally believe that women have the power to change the world. I see this in myself too. Men have that power as well, and they can be our biggest supporters, but women possess a special type of inner strength and determination. We historically are nurturers, caretakers, and community builders. I don't want to perpetuate any stereotypes or generalizations, but I have personally noticed a tendency towards these characteristics.

While I don't have children myself, I find a strong need to nurture my own relationships and connect people with each other. I host a monthly ladies' night, and I love seeing women develop new friendships. I enjoy watching my own coaching clients blossom, from being anxious people who are afraid of celebrating their successes, to women who are confident in their abilities and able to articulate them eloquently during their sales calls.

The women I interact with are therapists, coaches, health-care professionals, authors, experts, and changemakers. They are young women who are just starting out in their career paths and possess an entrepreneurial fire. They are middle-aged women who feel a deep desire to create a legacy and leave the world a better place for their children.

Being able to give back in a significant way motivates my clients. If you stay small and are scared of bringing out your power to the world, then you will always be afraid of truly making your mark on the world. And the planet desperately needs your unique talents, strengths, and insights. We need more healing and community. And women entrepreneurs have the skills and power to make that change happen.

I want to create a ripple effect of women empowering each other to succeed and to give women the tools they need to be more successful, so they can pass on this goodness and prosperity overall. When we are able to heal ourselves and the planet, we will create some phenomenal change.

I also have a personal mission to empower women because I struggled quite a bit when I was a young girl, and later as a young woman. I felt unsure of myself in the world and was scared of bringing out my power. Others took advantage of me and I experienced many different traumas that made me question my worth. My previous lack of self-esteem also led to making some poor financial decisions which reflected my own struggle with confidence.

It's easier to see the beauty and power in other people than in ourselves. Let's change that perception! Owning your power and being secure in your own strengths doesn't start with comparing yourself to other people. It begins by believing in yourself and in your capabilities.

Sales is a skill that you can learn. It's not something which naturally comes to everyone. But once you integrate a script and structure into your routine and practice that method with a strong mindset foundation, you will make sales. You will be able to genuinely connect with people, and you don't have to feel as though you need to manipulate someone or use cheesy sales tactics in order for them to believe in you and your services.

You can really just be yourself during the whole process. You can own that power and bring it out naturally.

A brief word about the structure of this book. I've written it as a six-week challenge with a week being Monday through Friday. For each of the five days, you will read a short chapter and complete an exercise. I know that you're a busy woman and I do not want to overwhelm you with too many tasks each day.

Here is what I cover in each week:

Week One is about your perception of sales, mindset, your values, and getting to the heart of what you want.

Week Two dives into getting clear on your ideal customer as well as tackling beliefs that may hold you back.

Week Three addresses pricing, the importance of creating a sales script, and the first section of your sales script.

Week Four moves into the second section of your sales script and the elements to include.

Week Five encourages you to practice your sales script and develop a rock-solid follow-up process with your prospects.

Week Six is geared towards developing a resilient mindset, dealing with ghosted clients, and determining what you truly want for your business.

I hope you find this material helpful in your personal journey. Feel free to email me at jula.pereira@gmail.com and tell me what originally drew you to this book. I am happy to assist you with any sales questions you may have.

Thank you again for letting me be a part of your sales journey. Here's to your success.


Jula Pereira

# Week 1

# Day 1: Redefining Sales

What do you think of when you hear the word "sales?" You've probably done this exercise before, and most likely you conjured up the image of a slimy car salesman who frequently has to go back to their manager with your proposed price. When he comes back, you wonder if he even went to the manager in the first place or if he visited the break room and helped himself to one of the donuts on the table instead. In fact, when I purchased my Nissan Leaf, I was so disgusted by the back-and-forth fake sales process that in the end, I was willing to sign anything to zoom out of there in my new electric vehicle.

Unfortunately, sales have gotten a bad rap in our modern culture. Many people have the perception that sales equals manipulation, dishonesty, unethical behavior, domination, fear, you name it. You've probably thought the same idea before because unfortunately, there are a lot of salespeople who are obsessed with competition and want to make the sale at any cost. They approach sales with only money as the end goal, and they will say anything and do anything to get the close.

The hard sell is not how a lot of women operate. Sure, I've met ambitious women who wanted to make their mark in the world, but just because you are ambitious and have big financial goals doesn't mean that you have to adopt the "to the death" mentality when it comes to selling. In fact, women who take on this more competitive edge often do so at the expense of their health, ethics, and overall happiness. Perhaps they can keep up with the boys, but the cost of the competition is immense. And who wants to pass these principles onto their kids anyway?

The first step in changing your relationship with sales is to change the way you see sales. If you see sales as a game, a battle, or anything else that has that type of connotation, you will approach your sales calls and meetings prepped for a fight. You will unintentionally create a shield around yourself and will feel the need to defend yourself when someone has a simple objection. That defender is not who you are as a person - it's just a mask that you wear.

If you approach sales with a different mindset, you'll automatically have more relaxed connections with your prospective clients. You don't even have to try to prove your point to them. You can be more natural, more yourself. And that feeling is what you want to bring to your sales calls. When you're just being yourself, people trust you and see you for who you are. It's very true that people buy from those they know and like. So, show your true self and don't worry about just making the sale.

One of my mentors told me that he doesn't like to call them "sales calls." He prefers the term "service calls." I really connected with that new terminology. When I think of being of service to someone, I genuinely want to help them. With the idea of service in mind from the very first interaction, you no longer feel the need to manipulate someone to purchase your product.

When you ask a potential client the right questions, you will simultaneously demonstrate your expertise as well as get into the heart of their struggle and situation. Be an investigator, uncovering the heart and depth of their need, and only then will you be able to see whether or not you can help them.

There's no need to be nervous about your calls. You're doing an act of service! You already are a helper and you enjoy giving your clients the best service possible. So, use that same mentality to help out your prospective clients too. Unlike the slimy car salesmen, the goal is not to get the client to sign on the dotted line and take their money. The goal is actually to help them - whether or not they buy from you.

I've had many instances in my business where I've actually turned down clients or referred them out because after asking the right questions, I realized that I couldn't help them. I am a very honest person, and I like to be direct with people.

Just the other day, a non-profit asked whether I could provide them a social media management and email marketing package. My team has plenty of experience with social media, and we could easily whip out content for that task, no problem. We don't specialize, however, in email marketing and would have to hire a white labeler for that particular service. On top of that, I was moving into my new sales and coaching business and wasn't doing as much social media anymore, so the project didn't excite me.

I could have easily hired someone to do the service as a white labeler and marked up the price in order for my company to make a profit from this deal, but I refused. Instead, I told the prospective client that they could get the same service directly from the white labeler and I gave her my colleague's information.

Was that lost potential income? Sure thing. But I felt good about saying no because I knew it would open the door to what I really wanted to do - coach women entrepreneurs in overcoming their fear of sales and partnering with other people who needed done-for-you sales help.

When your focus is not just about the money and it's more about how you treat people, you can step back and take a deep breath. You don't have to prove yourself to anyone. Start to redefine the word "sales" in your own mind to be the equivalent of serving, giving, assisting, helping. In this way you will change your whole perception of sales and how you relate to your prospective client. You are not trying to prove yourself to anyone. And there's no game. Just honesty.

Many of the women entrepreneurs I meet really just want to be honest and straightforward with their prospective clients. They don't want to manipulate them with false scarcity tactics or flash action bonuses. They just want to be real on their sales calls and help whoever is in front of them.

When you are able to authentically be yourself on your sales calls, assertively and confidently sell your services, not give into people's demands, and see your sales calls as a two-way interview where you also determine whether you want to work with the prospective client, then you are on your way to re-defining your relationship with sales.

**Your Turn**

*Draw a line vertically down a piece of paper or in your journal and make two columns. Label the first column "What I Grew Up Believing About Sales" and the second column "How I Redefine Sales."*

*In the first column write all the negative words you thought about sales. Some examples include "manipulative" and "conniving." In the second column, write your new perception of sales such as "genuine" and "helpful."*

*Take a moment to compare the two columns. Cross out the negative words on the left-hand column and circle or star the ones on the right. Close your eyes for a moment and begin to visualize yourself embodying the positive words in the right column.*

# Day 2: Redefining Your Mindset

The foundation for your business and your life is a solid mindset. Having a strong mindset is incredibly important, especially as an entrepreneur, because you will eventually need to weather the ups and downs which are bound to happen in your business. No entrepreneur is immune to the rough patches, but it's all about how you view them and handle them which will make or break you.

If you have a strong mindset which keeps you focused, calm, and enthusiastic, it doesn't mean that you will never feel any emotions. I still get angry, frustrated, sad (often with tears), or afraid. Just the other day, I had a series of sales calls and every single person either did not show up or said no to me. I walked into my boyfriend's office and cried in his arms. But afterwards, I felt better and I let it go. I carried on with my day, soothed by Joerg's hug. When your mindset is strong, you will be able to feel things deeply but also let them go more easily. You won't have to ruminate on the past.

Previously, I was a counselor for emotionally disturbed teenage girls who were constantly in a state of emotional flux. My fellow counselor Ali taught them the word "impervious." The Merriam Webster dictionary defines *impervious* as "not capable of being affected or disturbed." Ali explained to those girls, "If you are impervious to life's situations, then you can handle them better." In sales and in business, this word is such a good reminder. You won't sweat the small stuff and when the big stuff comes along, you'll be able to meet those challenges with grace and smoothness.

How do you develop this impervious mindset? How do you protect yourself from having three bad days in a row if a not-so-ideal situation unfolds in your business? The trick is having a daily mindset routine.

When my sales coach told me that I needed to develop a mindset routine, I jumped into the task with full force. He suggested several things that I could do: I could write in my journal, create a gratitude list, visualize my success, read inspiring stories from people who overcame hardships, meditate, or watch uplifting commencement speeches. Or I could do all of the above.

I chose all of the above.

I was so determined to change my mindset. I was like a soldier in boot camp, and I religiously tried to do every single thing on the list every day. He even had me visualize myself closing the deal before my sales calls and putting on some invigorating music to pump me up. I chose the song "Glorious," by Macklemore. To this day, I can feel my heart pumping fast as I recall the lyrics of the song, "I feel glorious, glorious/ Got a chance to start again!"

But instead of feeling like I could conquer the world, I felt extremely anxious inside. I was worried that I wasn't doing the exercises perfectly and the techniques weren't "working." I watched some of my classmates in my Facebook Ads Agency program excel at their sales calls and score $10k deals while I struggled to close any of my calls. I felt extremely defective, like there was something permanently wrong with me.

In order to overcome these feelings of inadequacy, I had to let go of trying to find the "right" way to do things. I got back to the basics and listened to my gut on what felt appropriate for where I was at. I told myself that I was enough. I sought out therapy and learned how to nurture the little girl inside me and comfort her when she needed help. From this place of self-care, I also found the two mindset routines which support me to this day: doing a gratitude journal and meditating for 5-10 minutes.

For my gratitude journal, I focused on writing down both the small and big things for which I felt grateful. My individual gratitudes could be as simple as having a warm, delicious meal to eat or bigger achievements, such as closing a $10k deal. I listed at least six items each time because that way, I knew I had to dig a bit deeper to find those areas which might not seem as obvious.

With meditation, I used an app to sink into a guided meditation. I purposefully kept it 5-10 minutes long because I knew I could commit to this task and I felt extremely relaxed after such a short period of time. I personally connected with the guided meditations because I could let go more easily and focus on the soothing voice on the other end. But I also found that setting a timer for that short amount and paying attention to my breathing did wonders for my mindset.

Many women are super-busy moms, partners, and professionals. When I bring up the topic of creating a mindset routine, many of them are either resistant to the idea or they cannot imagine having the time to do them. "I already wake up so early trying to get the kids to school," they say. Another common reason is, "It's a luxury for me to take a shower. How am I going to find 30 minutes for meditating?"

First of all, let's get one thing clear. You don't have to do it all. You don't need to be perfect. Your sales process is not a competition and you aren't running a race. You are learning to take care of yourself. We all know and love the metaphor that you need to put on your own oxygen mask before you can help anyone else. It's so true! You won't be as effective a businesswoman, mom, friend, partner, wife, or colleague if you can't take care of yourself.

Secondly, all I'm asking of you is 5-10 minutes of your day. In Gay Hendrickson's book *The Big Leap,* he talks about time being an illusion. When we are in the middle of an activity that produces a sense of flow, time seems to go quickly. When we do something that we dislike, time seems to take forever. We're caught in this cycle, thinking that we can either beat the clock or that we're constantly racing against time.

If you knew an endeavor was important to you, you would make time for it. Take my goal of writing a book. I procrastinated for at least three months before I committed to a writing schedule. Now I write every morning, Monday through Friday, for thirty minutes a day, starting at 8:00 am. I have the goal to compose at least 1,000 words each day.

I thought I didn't have the time to write a book because I have a busy schedule of sales calls, networking, and other meetings. But the fact of the matter was that I was actually just scared of getting started. I was terrified of revealing myself and potentially failing or getting rejected. So, I didn't create the time I needed to make writing a priority.

Another benefit of having a strong, impervious mindset is that you'll view rejection differently on your sales calls. You won't take "no" so personally, and you can more easily move onto your next prospective client. Women entrepreneurs tell me all the time that they are afraid of rejection and that it hurts their feelings when someone doesn't want to work with them. But when someone says no to you, they are actually doing you a favor.

What do I mean by that statement? When a person chooses another route, you potentially avoid working with someone who wasn't a good fit for you, and they unintentionally save you months of headaches. Maybe they were a high-maintenance client. Perhaps they were a cheapskate who would not value what you had to offer. Or when they said "no" to you, it opened the opportunity for the right, high-paying client to come along, someone who truly needed your services and became a raving fan.

If your mindset is in the right place, you wouldn't let one little "no" affect you in any major way. That "no" just means that you are one step closer to a "yes." Sales doesn't have to be a do-or-die situation. When your mind is in a good place and you feel utterly confident and passionate about your services, you're not going to let one small rejection affect you. You'll actually perceive it in a whole new light, and you'll be pumped up to take your next call.

This positive mindset is the incentive for spending your 5-10 minutes per day doing your mental exercises. These moments will have a lasting effect, not only on your sales calls, but on your busy, crazy life; those times you find out your kid is eating dirt, you have to wait on the phone for a Comcast rep, or you don't have a tampon in your purse when your period unexpectedly starts flowing. Your mindset is there to support you during the moments you are about to pitch your high-ticket offer or you have to deal with unexpected changes in your life.

I recommend starting your mindset routine with the two simple practices which changed my own life: a gratitude journal and a short meditation session. Once you have tried these two practices for a while and have realized that they may not be exactly the right fit for you, then you can explore other avenues for enhancing your mindset: watching inspiring videos, listening to motivating podcasts, spending time in prayer if you are spiritually-minded, writing in your journal, or reading a passage from a heartfelt book.

**Your Turn: Developing a Mindset Routine**

*Set aside 5-10 minutes per day for your new mindset routine. Put it down in your calendar just like any other to-do item. If you are a morning person, you can try waking up 10 minutes early to do your routine. If tend to be more of a night owl, you can do your routine right before you go to bed.*

*Choose between the following two options:*

*1. Write six things you are grateful for every day.*

*2. Meditate by closing your eyes and paying attention to your inhales and exhales.*

*For the gratitude journal, I purchased a beautiful notebook dedicated to this practice. You can start with small things like a hot cup of tea, the smell of your baby's head, or walks with your dog around the block. Mix it up with the bigger achievements, like reaching your yearly business goals or recovering from an illness.*

*For the meditation option, I use an app which provides guided meditations. Some people respond to those better than trying to sit quietly on their own. Don't judge yourself for thinking during your meditations or being distracted. Set a timer and start out with five minutes.*

*I've purposefully only given you two options here to choose from because I don't want to overwhelm you! At some point, you can experiment with other mindset practices and tools, such as writing down your wins for the week and posting them on social media in order to stay accountable (I call these my #FridayWins). But for now, try out one of these practices and see how they go.*

# Day 3: Regulating Your Emotions

Throughout this process, you will experience some days when you feel strong and self-assured in your mindset. Other days, you'll have a series of people tell you that they don't want your services and that rebuff will be difficult to take in. Life will throw you a series of curve balls, but you don't have to be a slave to your reactions in the process.

As an entrepreneur, you're going to inevitably go through periods of ups and downs. When I decided to build an agency for myself and increase my prices, I felt elated when I closed a couple of deals. But I quickly realized, as I tried to fulfill those deals that I was in way over my head. Some of the expectations didn't come to fruition, and I lost those clients. My elation turned into depression as the pendulum completely swung the other way.

Sometimes you'll have a good cash flow going and you'll experience a lot of growth. Other times in your career, it will seem as though you can't close any of the prospective clients who come to you. What's most important in the process is to maintain your perspective and keep going. Your emotions may swing through extremes, but I found that it's best not to give either your elation or your depression too much power.

Meditation and mindfulness have helped me with these emotional extremes and so has therapy. Using those tools, I am able to maintain a steady stream and not let circumstances affect me as often. If you're able to regulate your emotional reactions to various situations you will be able to find a way to deal with the heart of the problem rather than exacerbating the issue in front of you.

Here's a little tip that I've learned - venting to your partner, spouse, or girlfriends doesn't really help in regulating your emotions. You may feel a temporary sense of relief in that moment and you may feel a release moving those emotions out of your system, but you can also find yourself persisting in those emotions and sensations.

Also, when you vent to someone, it's easier to take on the role of the victim and to blame someone else for making you experience your current feelings. You actually have the control over feeling a certain way. No one else has that power over you. I know this is hard to remember because I also tend to blame others first when I'm in a tough situation. But when I step back and re-evaluate where I am, then my emotions can shift.

Breathing intentionally and taking a time-out helps to dissipate negative thoughts and challenge unpleasant emotions. Celebrating your wins allows you to gain the perspective which you need in the moment. Instead of focusing on the bad occurrences that happen or go wrong, make a mental note of the circumstances you are grateful for. It's hard to be upset when you remind yourself of what you are thankful for and what you've accomplished so far.

As you are going through this mindset work which includes all the ups and downs, learn to be gentle with yourself. We are our own worst critics. Why do we tend to be so hard on ourselves all the time? I see this happen with a lot of women and I've noticed this judgment in myself as well.

It's honestly impossible to fulfill the superwoman ideal. You're not going to live up to some unreachable standard of perfectionism. No one has a 100% closing rate! It's not realistic to think that way and trying to be a superwoman puts a lot of pressure on you.

You are an amazing entrepreneur and you have great attributes to share with this world. You have unique gifts and talents that only come from you. Your purpose is your own. Don't be so hard on yourself. I had to learn this lesson again and again. When I made mistakes, I used to chastise and talk down to myself. This negative self-talk made me nervous and depressed.

But when I learned how to be gentler with myself and nurture myself the way a mother would with her child, I also learned to forgive my mistakes or to laugh the incident off. I don't want to be perfect because then there's no reason for me to grow and learn. When I see my friends or my partner stumbling, I don't judge them as harshly as I once judged myself.

Be kind to yourself. It goes a long way.

### Your Turn: Regulate Your Emotions

*The next time that you feel frantic or upset, take a few deep breaths and pause. If you are sitting down, stand up. Take a few minutes to write a list of what you are grateful for and review that list in the moment. How does it make you feel to read that list?*

# Day 4: Your Core Values

Now that you have a different perspective on sales and have started your daily mindset routine, let's talk about another topic that's truly fundamental. Many women entrepreneurs make a vital mistake about getting wrapped up in marketing themselves and nailing their sales scripts before they ask themselves some very basic questions. The most essential question that you need to ask yourself is, "What do I really want?" The second most useful question is, "What are my core values in my business and my life?

Your core values define who you are as an individual and what you believe in. They will be your guiding principles which assist you in which deals or offers you want to say yes to and which ones do not resonate with your purpose. By knowing your core values, you can begin to build your business from a place of abundance, prosperity, and ease rather than, "I should do this." You know that you are not compromising yourself and can draw appropriate boundaries.

When you approach sales from a self-empowered place, standing up for yourself and creating good boundaries, you're automatically going to know through-and-through what you are worth. Your core values create a solid foundation of strength and confidence upon which you can rely. You don't have to bargain with prospective clients or get down on your knees to accommodate everyone when you refuse to compromise your core values.

Like does attract like. So, when you come from a place of desperation for money and fear that no one is ever going to sign up for your services, guess who's going to be lurking around the corner? A bunch of prospective clients who are quick to invalidate your expertise and cause you to second-guess yourself.

But you don't have to settle for clients who don't appreciate your worth. There is an essential factor that creates the foundation for your business and your life. It's your core values. Your core values represent who you are on a very deep level and they speak volumes about who you are as a person and what you believe in profoundly. When you have this inner compass in place, it is easier to orient yourself to the right direction in your journey and to identify the people who do not resonate with you. You'll be able to tell in the interviewing process who you click with and who could potentially be a red flag for you.

When I began to figure out my core values, I had a hard time narrowing my focus. I had several subsets of values and realized that I could group a number of them together. For example, authenticity is one of my top core values. But underneath authenticity, I chose to include transparency, honesty, and follow-through, which I call reliability. Authenticity seemed to encompass all those values and it acts as a guiding light for both my business and my life.

What do you value and how can you determine this for yourself? The first step is to identify certain qualities that you've noticed other people complimenting you for. Maybe you repeatedly get comments that you are a good listener, a dedicated worker, or an empathetic or loyal person. Start to think about who you are objectively and jot down a few ideas. You can also ask some close family members and friends to give you valuable feedback.

Think about certain situations that have come up repeatedly in your life and how you chose to handle them. What makes you feel invigorated, inspired, and hopeful? I decided for myself that generosity was one of my core values because I always want to be helpful to my family, friends, clients, and community. It is important for me to make a good income and donate to causes I believe in because I want to contribute to making the world a better place.

Here are the six core values which I live by:

1. Authenticity
2. Self-Care
3. Compassion
4. Generosity
5. Gratitude
6. Fun

I added fun at the end of my list because I didn't want to interact with clients in a dull way. I want to have fun in everything I do. I enjoy singing and learning new songs on my ukulele, laughing and cracking jokes with clients and team members, going out swing dancing with my partner, and hiking among beautiful California redwoods. Life doesn't always have to be serious, and I want my core values to reflect that as well.

If a certain attribute is important to you, then you will see if these qualities are reflected in prospective clients during your sales calls. If I'm on a call with someone who is completely monotone and boring or doesn't have any outside interests besides working 24/7, they are probably not going to be the best client for me. They can have all the money in the world to pay me for my services, but because they don't match my core value of fun, it won't be a long-term, fulfilling relationship.

Start to view your core values as your roadmap and let them act as a guide for you.

Self-care is especially important for me. I get massages once or twice a month, do yoga every Sunday with my dread-headed Rastafarian teacher from Venezuela, and try to go jogging with my partner several times a week. I eat good, organic, mostly vegan food. I meditate most days with my Calm app. I want to take care of my body and mental health because that way I can serve more people and inspire others to do the same.

Your core values may come up casually in a conversation, or you can intently look for signs of matching values when you talk to someone on the phone or in person. Don't take your core values for granted. And when you commit to several specific values on paper and are able to tell people what they are, you will find yourself internalizing them and acting on them differently.

It's fantastic to have a set of core values written down, but it's important to commit to practicing them in your daily life. By writing down your core values and committing them to memory, you can start to internalize them. When certain situations arise, ask yourself if they resonate with your core values. You will have an opportunity to mentally determine if the situation at hand aligns with your values.

I have to admit that there are times when I could be more compassionate with myself or other people. I'm quick to feel annoyed or judgmental. But when I remember that compassion is one of my core values, it inspires me to look beyond the temporary, fleeting emotion and put myself in another person's shoes. I can have compassion for a client who expresses fear of changing or believing in herself because I've been in her situation too.

One more point to remember: identifying your core values and then living them out can be challenging when you are faced with difficult situations. But having your values in place also comes in handy when you're in those exact circumstances because you can use them as a guidepost.

For example, I was offered to do sales coaching for an acquaintance's online program. He wanted me to teach his students twice a week and offered to pay my normal rate. On the surface, the job seemed ideal. However, when I ran through his content, I realized that his sales tactics did not align with my own core values. I did not feel as though I would live up to my core value of authenticity, which for me includes integrity and honesty, if I accepted the position.

I turned down the offer, but within an hour, I closed with another coaching client who actually was in complete alignment with my values. The universe was making a statement to me, rewarding me for trusting my gut at that moment and not compromising my core values!

### *Your Turn: Identifying Your Core Values*

*List 15 to 20 values which you believe define you on a deep level. Think about the different areas of your life related to family, work, friends, and your community. What defines you? What do you deeply believe? What can you not live without in your life? Don't worry if you can't think of that many. That may just mean that you have already narrowed down what is truly valuable to you.*

*Now examine your list and circle five or six of the values which you believe truly speak to your heart and define your core self. Start sharing this list with your partner, close friends, and team to get their feedback. Ultimately, you have to be comfortable with your list because this is a personal exercise, but sometimes it's good to get other's feedback. They can often see traits about you which you cannot see yourself.*

*Once you are happy with the list of core values, write them down and post them in a prominent place. Internalize them and begin to tell other people about your list. You will start to get more confident in your values each day.*

# Day 5: What Do You Want for Your Business?

Once you have your core values internalized, it's time to start thinking about the foundation of your business and the ultimate question: "What do you want?" Everyone has different needs and visions for your business. There isn't a right or wrong answer. You're the creator, designer, and implementer of your business and you should always remember that. Don't let someone else dictate who or what you should be. There is no "should" in this context!

You may be a mom with two young kids, so working 10 hours per week is ideal for your schedule. You may be an ambitious woman who's always dreamed of having a high-ticket offer and being an influencer to thousands with your life-changing coaching program. Maybe you enjoy one-on-one work with your clients rather than being in front of a group. Or perhaps you want to work a full 40-hour week and have a small team of two or three people who assist you with sales calls, administrative work, and social media management.

When I joined a $10k program, I bought into the idea that I needed to make $100k per month as an agency owner in order to be seen as "successful." I got caught up in their hype, though I didn't realize it at the time. I tried my hardest to really make their definition of success happen. I launched a funnel to get leads and hopped on back-to-back sales calls. But in reality, I was following someone else's dream. I was convinced it was the right path for me, but in actuality, their dream didn't make me feel happy, excited, or passionate. In fact, all I felt was anxiety and fear.

It's okay to feel a little fear but to experience the unknown anyway. We wouldn't start new ventures if we always listened to our fears. But there's a difference between feeling a bit nervous about building your business and experiencing full-on anxiety because you're just doing what someone told you that you should be doing. If you dig deep and listen to what your heart and soul are desperately trying to tell you, you will find the answer yourself.

When I start to work with new women entrepreneurs in my coaching practice, I ask them this simple question, "What do you love to do?" Usually, I get answers of what people think that they are good at rather than what they are really passionate about. The women who come to me have had varied careers and they have tried many different paths. Sure, they are perfectly competent in many areas and have developed interesting skill sets. Heck, even I was a massage therapist at one point and a loan officer at another! It took me some time to learn exactly what I felt passionate about and I learned so much about myself with each experience.

But the question, "What do you love to do?" is really a show stopper because it makes you sit back and think deeply about what gets you excited in the morning. And when you are able to genuinely and honestly answer that question, then you are ready to find your niche for your business. Having a niche will help you clarify exactly where you take your business - whether you want to keep it at $25,000 per year as a part-time gig or whether you are ready to scale up to a $2 million per-year company with 25 employees.

In my own journey, I thought that I could wear multiple hats at once; in fact, most business owners who are just starting out actually need to perform many different roles because they are typically a one-woman show. I had a background in holistic healing, art, customer service, writing, sales, social-media management, advertising, funnel building, hiring teams, and managing teams. Whew! It feels exhausting just listing all of those out. Sure, I could create audiences and launch an ad campaign on Facebook, but did that make me happy? No way!

I realized that I was happiest when I was around people, interacting with them, networking and listening to stories. I was curious about their lives and genuinely wanted to help them. I was a master networker and knew how to assess someone's needs and connect them to the exact person to help them. People showed their gratitude when I connected them with the right person or service. I loved every moment of that.

And that's when it dawned on me - I am a people connector rather than an implementer of technical knowledge. That's why sales comes so naturally to me. And I absolutely love to teach. I really enjoy watching people's faces light up when they get clarity on their own situations or implement something new and find success in that. I enjoy speaking to audiences and engaging them in different exercises. In essence, I'm passionate about being a teacher, coach, sales professional, networker, and writer. So that passion is what I've decided to build my business around.

So, what do you love? What are you extremely good at in your business which also makes you happy? What population do you enjoy serving the most? What type of business do you want to create? Do you want to stay small or do you want to change millions of lives? Do you want to work only with women? Do you feel very passionate about a certain cause and want to donate a percentage of your proceeds to it through your business?

It's time to get to know yourself and give yourself permission to ask what you truly want. If you can't envision this business, you won't be able to manifest it as you want. And if you are not clear about what you want, then your sales process will stagnate as well. When I thought that I needed to make $100k per month as an agency owner, my sales calls were filled with my unspoken anxiety. And believe me, prospective clients can smell that a mile away! They want to stay as far away as possible from someone who does not exude confidence and leadership. They need to trust you, and it starts when you trust yourself.

Trusting yourself means that you will also learn to trust your process. I struggled with finding my specialty for a very long time. In fact, I thought initially that staying a generalist would actually be more beneficial because I could keep my options open and I wouldn't put myself in a box. When I started my social-media marketing business, I said yes to every single person who willingly paid my $300 per month miniscule package. So, I ended up working with non-profits, chiropractors, wineries, real-estate agents, and a whole slew of other random people.

The problem with staying broad is that it's really hard to market yourself to clients. I've met women entrepreneurs who tell me that their product or service is good for everyone and that's their market. Are you saying that your business can equally help a 13-year-old teenage boy who grew up in a privileged neighborhood in L.A. and an 89-year-old woman who never used a computer in her life? Scaling down your focus will allow you to get crystal clear on your message to a particular population, and then you can more successfully sell your product or service to them.

When you're not clear on who you want to serve and what you are passionate about, your marketing will have no focus or impact. Once you have a clear idea of what you are passionate about and what makes you get out of bed excited in the morning, you can use this vision to set realistic 30, 60, and 90-day goals. You can start to spend some time visualizing the business of your dreams and how many people you are going to help.

You can start to approach your sales calls differently, armed with the knowledge of both your core values and what you want to create for yourself. It will change your relationship with the word "no" because in essence, you don't want to work with anyone who doesn't click with you and your vision for yourself. You only need to serve people who fulfill this higher purpose and your calling.

### *Your Turn: What Do You Want?*

*Take out a piece of paper or your journal and start to free-write ideas concerning what you are passionate about in your business and what you want it to look like. Answer the following questions:*

1. *What do you love doing? What is your primary role in the business?*

2. *What are your skills and strengths? What are tasks you want to outsource?*

3. *How much income do you want to make per month?*

4. *How many team members do you want to have?*

5. *How many hours per week do you want to work?*

6. *Who do you enjoy serving the most? What types of people would you not mind saying no to on sales calls?*

7. *What would you do with your free time outside of the business if things ran smoothly and you reached the level of success you seek?*

# Week 2

# Day 6: Who Is Your Ideal Customer?

It's really common, in my opinion, for entrepreneurs to not know who exactly they want to serve. I see this issue all the time. Many people think that they should serve everyone and their mother. That lack of focus makes your marketing incredibly difficult. You have to craft so many messages and appeal to so many types of people. If you narrowed down your ideal customer, you would then be able to hone in on those person's pain points, needs, dreams, and desires, so your message to them would be quite different.

Let's say that I told everyone I was a coach who helped men and women. That's quite a broad range of people! How do I speak to a woman versus a man? Which platforms would I hang out on social media? I would absolutely drive myself crazy because I didn't have a laser-sharp focus for my business. I wouldn't know which networking groups to go to, which social media posts would be the most effective, or how I should craft my messaging.

Now, the reality is that I know my niche audience very well. I am a sales coach and I cater to service-based, women entrepreneurs like therapists, coaches, authors, experts, consultants, and changemakers. The age range for the women I work with does vary, however I tend to attract women with young children who want to integrate their businesses with their family lives. I also attract ambitious women who earn six-figures or more per year and need to hire and train a reliable sales team to promote and expand their high-ticket coaching programs. See how specific those two ideal clients are?

Another reason that you should be as clear as possible about your ideal clients is that this focus will make your sales calls much easier to execute. Why is that? Because you will be able to identify on the phone through a series of strategic questions whether or not the person fits within your vision of an ideal customer. Of course, nothing is perfect and the prospective client may not have all the qualities you are looking for. But if they share similar core values, exemplify the type of person you are happiest serving, and are willing and eager to pay your fees, you've found a gem.

When I do sales for agencies, I always look out for red flags because I'm really gauging in my sales calls whether or not a person is a good fit for the company. Can we serve this person? Will we be able to get the results that they are looking for? How is their communication? Will they potentially be a high-maintenance client? When you ask the right questions, you should pay close attention to the answers.

You probably wouldn't put down "high-maintenance" as one of the qualities of your ideal client. Rather, you're looking out for people who are pleasant to work with, have a need that you know you can fulfill, and enthusiastically sign up for your services with minimal convincing. In other words, these people will sell themselves on your service or program!

Many marketing courses teach you how to make an "avatar." This is just a fancy word for an imaginary profile of your ideal client. You want to make this client as detailed as possible to give it life. You can mimic your avatar by comparing it to one of your real-life, close-to-ideal clients or you can use your imagination. Give your avatar a name and be specific on their age, occupation, family life, leisure activities, and lifestyle habits.

Here's an example of one of my avatars:

*Amber has been a helper ever since she was a child. She is happily married and has two children ages ten and eight-years old. She has always wanted to be in a helping profession and chose to be a therapist because she had a difficult childhood and was able to overcome her past by seeking out therapy on her own. She just started her practice and is making about $3,000 per month.*
*She works about 10-15 hours per week between marketing, seeing her clients, and administrative work for charting, but she definitely has more room in her practice to grow.*

*She believes in the goodness of people and is extremely patient. She tends to say yes to many undertakings and has a hard time drawing appropriate boundaries with people. She is an environmentalist and wants to improve the planet, as well as help people in their time of suffering and need. She drives an electric vehicle and buys organic produce. She also is a believer in building community and regularly volunteers at the local hospice.*

*Amber is terrified of selling herself. The thought of promoting herself on social media or in networking meetings causes a cold sweat and her heart starts to race. She is extremely good at what she does and gets regular five-star reviews online. She knows that she has helped many women in her practice. However, she has a hard time telling people about these achievements.*

*When she was a child, she never boasted about herself, and she was often told to shut up and remain quiet. She got straight A's when she was younger and volunteered at the local hospital as a candy striper when she was in high school, but she never celebrated these wins. She tended to put more pressure on herself.*

*She is now in a position where she can take on new clients, but she tends to freeze on the phone and has noticed that her sales calls don't go very smoothly because she's so nervous. She's also afraid of public speaking.*

*Amber needs me to teach her how to be more confident on her sales calls. She wants me to help ease her nerves and guide her through ways to build up her selling abilities because she knows that this nervousness is her biggest roadblock. Once a client signs up with her, she is fine and knows what to do in order to get great results. It's just that she doesn't know how to get the clients in the first place. She would also love to learn how to celebrate her wins and be more vocal about them because she knows that this is an area she needs to improve upon. Lastly, she wants to have a marketing plan for the future and goals for herself.*

*Amber is afraid of being dependent on her husband's income alone. She was very independent before she met her husband, but when they got engaged, she decided to go back and get her master's degree. Her husband financially took care of her during that time, but she felt guilty about that. Now that she's licensed and their kids are older, she wants to start contributing more towards the household expenses. It's very expensive to have kids and she has to think about saving for their college educations as well. She also is afraid of going into credit-card debt again.*

*She wants me to know that she is motivated to change, even though she has a lot of fear. She also wishes for me to ease her apprehension around selling and reassure her that sales are not as big a deal as she makes them out to be. She wants me to know that she is extremely busy with her practice, as well as being a good wife and mom, but she knows this process is important and will make time for it.*

*She's a great listener because she's been trained as a therapist, and she loves reading self-help books. But she's also had a hard time applying that knowledge and being consistent. If she gains confidence in sales, she hopes to use those techniques of influence to be a better parent, friend, and wife by learning how to say no more easily.*

*In her free time, Amber enjoys hiking in beautiful locations, knitting sweaters, baking with her kids, and watching romantic comedies. She often makes dates with her girlfriends and they go to consignment stores or grab a coffee. She prioritizes her relationship with her husband and they try to go out on date nights as often as possible.*

See how detailed I got with my avatar? You can visualize exactly what type of person Amber is and what her pain points are. She is terrified of selling and public speaking, but she has a big heart and wants to help as many people as possible.

When you're clear on your ideal audience, not only will your marketing strategies become easier to formulate and execute, but your sales calls will get smoother as well because you can recognize promptly whether the prospective client falls in the category of your ideal client. The way the person answers your questions will show you whether or not they seem like a good person to onboard.

When you learn to say no to less-than-ideal clients, you open up opportunities for your ideal client to come along. If you are just starting your business, you will probably say yes to many clients because you want to bring in some revenue. This is perfectly okay. Over time, you will begin to refine your vision of what an ideal client looks like for you.

It's up to you whether you want to say "yes" to a prospective client. Remember that it's a two-way street. You are interviewing your prospective client as much as you they are interviewing you. At the end of the day, when you say yes to someone, you are inviting a learning experience.

Even if that client does not turn out to be ideal after all, you amass data which can be used in your sales process. You'll learn how to interpret potential red flags such as a client who demands that you discount your prices for them or someone who has a difficult time getting back to you. Remember that you are the creator of your business and you have the opportunity to manifest what you truly want.

### *Your Turn: Creating Your Own Avatar*

*Answer the following questions on a piece of paper or your journal in regards to your ideal customer or client:*

1. *What is your ideal customer's name?*

2. *How old are they?*

3. *What is their gender?*

4. *Are they married, in a partnership, or have children?*

5. *Where do they live? A suburban neighborhood or a big, bustling city?*

6. *What is their profession and how many hours per week do they work?*

7. *How much do they earn?*

8. *What do they like to do outside of work?*

9. *What do they read or watch on TV?*

10. *What are their deepest needs, pains, desires, and dreams?*

*Now create your own avatar profile using the answers to your questions. Make them as real as possible, as though they are actually someone you know.*

# Day 7: Letting Go of Control

If you have already started your business, you've probably quickly realized that often times you cannot hold on to certain outcomes. You will experience highs, when many people say yes to you on sales calls. You will also go through lows and find out that sometimes you can't help everyone or you have to deal with someone who won't pay you. Being an entrepreneur will challenge you to grow. It will test your limits. You will have to let go.

The most important point is to not getting too attached to certain situations, especially in the sales process. You can show up 100% to each of your sales calls but you cannot control whether or not someone will sign up to work with you. I like the saying, "When one door closes, another one opens." This idea allows me to keep perspective and not get too disappointed when something I want does not happen.

If you are clear about yourself and your capabilities, you will trust that the universe offers you exactly what you need at the exact time you need it. The process of sales is easier when you think this way because you stop taking outcomes so personally. When you realize that the universe works in your favor, you're able to regulate your emotions in a way that makes you productive rather than reactive. And you can keep your eye on the goal.

There are going to be times when you feel lost and uncertain and you want to control your outcome. When I was going after a $100k-per-month dream of having my own agency, I had a very limited definition of success. I worked so hard towards this goal that someone else created for me, but I didn't even realize that I was pursuing a dream that did not fit me. Then I put myself down for not making enough progress towards that fake goal.

When you let go of control, you can watch your own path unfold. There's a fine balance between striving to get everything just right by putting in extra effort versus learning to sit back and let events take their course. Believe me, you'll feel a lot less stressed about your business if you learn to take circumstances as they come and deal with problems in the moment, as they arise.

While you can take steps to plan and organize your life and business, you can't predict everything. It's a balancing act of staying motivated and in-tune with your short-term and long-term goals while flowing with the changes which life inevitably brings.

Trying to do everything yourself in your business can also be a symptom of wanting to control. In the beginning, you're most likely going to need to pull up your own bootstraps and be the marketer, salesperson, service provider, accountant, and whatever other role you have in your business.

But at some point, when you're ready, it's a great idea to ask for help, because otherwise, you'll be the bottleneck in your business, insisting everything needs to go through you first. You'll feel compelled to work all the time and believe that you are the best person for every job.

Letting go of control means that you can create space to breathe, relax, and de-stress. You can set out an intention but not be attached to any one outcome. You can learn how to delegate what you need to and still be satisfied with the results. You can also discover how to relax more and let the situations rise and fall.

### *Your Turn: Letting Go of Control*

*List all the things that you are responsible for at this time in your business. Circle the items which are actually not necessary for the success of your business. Next, put a check by the ones which can actually be delegated out to a virtual assistant or team member. Set up a plan on how you will delegate the check-marked items.*

## Day 8: Comparing Yourself to Others

When I was a kid, I often compared myself to my sister and brother. My sister had amazing math and science skills and got straight A's in school, while I felt inadequate with my A-'s and B+'s. My brother was the only boy in the family and he was the apple of my dad's eye. They had their own little club called the "Ju-Ju Boys." I often felt left out.

This feeling continued throughout my adolescent years. I remember buying those Teen Magazines and being fascinated by the perfect smiles of the white girls with blonde or brunette hair featured inside. I hated my skinny legs which I sometimes referred to as "chicken legs." Once a boy in my class said that he could easily snap my legs in half, and I was mortified. Being so thin, I didn't love myself fully.

I desperately wanted to belong. Because I felt really insecure inside, I constantly compared my own progress to other people's achievements. I enviously made checklists of all the qualities and traits they had which I didn't possess. I had a really hard time accepting myself for who I was or loving myself 100%.

Those feelings of insecurity haunted me even into my adult years when I started my business. There was one particular woman entrepreneur with whom I often compared myself. She was younger than me by more than a decade, but we started our businesses around the same time. She opted to drop out of college and pursued her business with full force. She also had a husband and two children. She was a powerhouse and she knew it.

I never exuded that level of confidence in my early twenties, and I certainly still struggled with it as a business owner. I was doing adequately with my social media marketing business, but I definitely wasn't growing my business as quickly as she was. She promptly amassed a team underneath her and then created and launched an online program. I obsessed while going through her social media threads, analyzing the beautiful branding photos and content she shared. She even opened up about how much money she earned.

It took me about a year to finally address my feelings of competition and insecurity around this person and realize what that envy did to myself and my own business. When you compare yourself to someone else's success and look at them with envy instead of admiration, the rivalry definitely gnaws away at your soul.

Envy over someone else's success causes you to get off-course from your own dreams and aspirations. You begin to think that you're not good enough or not deserving enough for success to happen in your life. Then the imposter syndrome creeps in as well, and you begin to feel as though you don't deserve to call yourself an expert in your field because you compare yourself to someone else's level of expertise. You start to believe that other people deserve love, success, and abundance, but you deserve nothing.

These feelings of inadequacy will definitely come through in your sales calls if you don't address them at the root. You will start to feel an internal pressure to act like someone you are not destined to be. I thought that I needed to be as successful as this woman in order for my business to be as admirable as hers. In actuality, she and I had very different trajectories, hopes, and dreams, and I really couldn't compare myself to her.

For example, I didn't want children and she ended up having them when she was young. I did not want to run a big team of people. Instead, I sought to build a business which would give me the freedom in my lifestyle to have a steady income while also spending time with my partner and friends. My definition of success, fulfillment, and balance just differed from hers.

When you compare yourself to other people and feel that pinch of envy over what they have, you also forget about the fact that everyone is on an individual journey. Your story is special and unique and so are your skill sets and passion. Everyone has a different zone of genius and each person has something to contribute to the world.

It was actually an internal struggle to decide how much of my story I should share. But in the end, I realized that by sharing it, I could benefit other women. Your story is your own, so come to terms with it. Your life path is your own, so claim it as something unique. You have many gifts to share in your business and there are prospective clients who desperately need what *you* have to offer, not the woman next door. So, don't give into the desire to compare your life to someone else's.

The best advice I got about not comparing myself to others was to instead focus on my own growth. I can compare myself to where I was even a year ago and marvel at the progress I've made in my life. I'm happy with how far I've come and glad that I don't have the tendency to compare myself to other people as much anymore. Yes, the feelings of envy still come up sometimes, but then they quickly fade away.

### *Your Turn: Overcoming the Need to Compare Yourself*

*Recall the person you were 10 years ago. What were you doing, thinking, and feeling back then? Write down five to ten things that you learned since then and see how far you've come. Circle the ones that you are particularly proud of.*

# Day 9: Imposter Syndrome

Imposter syndrome is the feeling of not being good enough to position yourself as a resource or expert in your business. These feelings can pop up whether you're just starting out in your business or whether you are making six or seven figures, and it can be exacerbated by feelings of inadequacy. These notions can come and go throughout your career, especially as you uplevel your business. The imposter syndrome is similar to comparing yourself to others because underneath all your success, you may not feel like you deserve it.

You may think that other people have their lives and businesses all figured out and that you're the only one who doesn't know what you're doing. People encourage you to, "Feel the fear and do it anyway," or "Fake it until you make it," and you try to do your best. But that feeling of being inadequate still haunts you.

I am here to tell you that most, if not all business owners experience imposter syndrome at some particular stage. It's easy to feel uncomfortable when you try something new and you have to find a way to exude confidence when you don't particularly feel it inside. There are probably little voices in your head saying, "Who do you think you are?" or "You don't have enough knowledge to call yourself an expert."

At the moments those voices arise, I stop myself and take a deep breath. Recognizing this tendency is the first step to dealing with the critical voices. Then, I actually have a conversation with these voices and give reasons why they are wrong. I speak to them as though they are separate people. I give examples of other ways I excelled at a job or attributes which bring me pride.

I definitely went through an on-again, off-again period of imposter syndrome, and I think that it's pretty common among entrepreneurs, in general. On the outside, male entrepreneurs seem to exude more confidence and bravado when they are just starting out, while women entrepreneurs often doubt themselves more. I think it's normal to have some self-doubt and it is not realistic to enter into a new venture without feeling some concerns. But if you let those fears cripple you, you'll never radiate the confidence you need in your sales process.

I had to do a lot of internal work in order to even start writing this book. I felt like an imposter giving advice to women entrepreneurs because I thought I needed to be in a more successful place before writing my advice in a book. There was a little voice in my head that was afraid that people would judge what I had to say, or even worse, that they would not even want to read my book at all. But I had to work through those feelings by accepting that I have something valuable to say, counteracting the voices in my head with self-supporting affirmations, and starting my daily writing practice.

Addressing the voices in your head and telling yourself that you are worthy and you are competent is an ongoing task. One day, you may feel incredibly confident. Other days, you may begin to doubt yourself again. The trick to developing confidence every day is to practice self-kindness and compassion. For me, I choose to celebrate my wins, both big and small. This practice has been something that I've done for about a year now, and it's changed my mindset in a very dramatic way.

I celebrate my wins by writing a list of things that I have accomplished through the years, then I revisit this list when I feel less confident on a particular day. I also post my weekly wins publicly on my social media profiles, summarizing the accomplishments I experienced throughout that particular week. I have to admit that some days I did not feel like posting anything at all. But celebrating even small wins helped me learn to acknowledge my own progress towards reaching my personal goals.

Remember the woman entrepreneur to whom I compared myself? She had an uncanny way of not apologizing for her successes. In fact, she boldly showed both gratitude and pride for the life that she created for herself. She wasn't afraid to toot her own horn a little bit. Her confidence showed that she could be genuinely proud of herself for accomplishing certain goals. More people will put their trust in her because she exudes that confidence. When you seek out a provider, you want someone to confidently lead you. Your prospective clients want you to lead them boldly, as well.

As women, we're often told that it's inappropriate to brag about our achievements. We're taught that we need to be humble all the time. That's a bunch of BS. You should be proud of yourself and your accomplishments. You should see every small win as a true victory. You will go through hardships and life lessons, yes, but through those trials you will also discover the strength, skills, and competence that you never knew you had.

Finally, it's a good idea to address your bouts of imposter syndrome as they crop up and nip them in the bud because they can actually affect your sales and pricing. If you don't think that you are worthy of a certain price, you won't be paid what you are worth. You'll discount your services more often or give things away for free instead of creating the right boundaries. Tell yourself that you're going to wait for someone to come along who values your worth and happily pays your prices.

When you feel like an imposter, you might feel uncomfortable during your sales calls and will subconsciously avert the sale when you try to raise your prices to a decent level. Don't let these feelings hinder your success, because deep-down inside, you know what you are worth. It's time to let go of the self-criticism and own that power within you.

### *Your Turn: Counteracting Imposter Syndrome*

*In your journal, write down ten of your major successes that you are proud of. They can be small wins or big wins, but the important thing is to think deeply about your personal and professional accomplishments so you can own them.*

*Read over your list when you start to feel that sense of self-doubt or the twinge of imposter syndrome. Over time, it will be easier to claim these accomplishments with pride. Here's an example of my list:*

1. *Closed over $258,000 in new business over the course of a year for myself and other agencies through my authentic sales techniques.*
2. *Built a close community of friends.*
3. *Manifested a loving partnership and we've been together seven years.*
4. *Healed my relationship with my parents.*

5. *Ran straight for 45 minutes without stopping, averaging 4.2 miles each time.*
6. *Took up the ukulele and learned to sing and play songs within three months.*
7. *Coached many women entrepreneurs to feel more confident in their sales process.*
8. *Began to write my book after years of wanting to be an author.*
9. *Built up a profitable business after getting laid off.*
10. *Learned to love myself for who I am.*

**Bonus Exercise:** *At the end of the week. I like to write out a list of my accomplishments for the week and post them on social media. I call them my #FridayWins. It's great to read the supportive comments from other people. Making your achievements public also counteracts the deeply instilled belief that sharing your successes automatically means you are bragging.*

*Try your own #FridayWins post and list five to eight accomplishments you are especially proud of for the week. Even if this invitation feels uncomfortable at first, challenge yourself.*

# Day 10: Overcoming Limiting Money Beliefs

My parents often fought about money when I was a kid. My dad got extremely irritated with my mom's love of shopping and complained about the clutter in the house. As a young girl, I was imprinted with the unconscious belief that money causes strife and hardship in relationships. I was also a naturally frugal person, even as a girl. I remember how my dad asked my brother and me to pick out anything we wanted in a toy store and I refused. Part of me didn't think that I deserved anything. The other part of me felt that it was a waste, probably because I already had so many other toys which were perfectly fine.

I struggled with getting paid well after I graduated from college. I had no idea what it meant to negotiate my salary because I didn't have any role models who taught me those lessons. My mom retired from her preschool teaching job making $12 per hour. It was difficult for me to imagine myself making a lot of money because I was convinced you had to have a professional degree in order to do that. Many of my fellow second-generation Indian counterparts happily moved forward with their engineering, medical, or law degrees. But there I was, with my Comparative Literature degree, completely clueless on how to find a job or negotiate a decent salary.

My first full-time job at a group home for emotionally disturbed teenage girls brought me a whopping rate of $8.50 per hour. My next job as a part-time "temporary" typist earned me about $12 per hour, and they kept me as at temp for four years so they conveniently would not have to pay any benefits. I struggled with part-time and per diem jobs before I tried unsuccessfully to build my first business as a holistic healer. When I got married, my husband at the time didn't make a lot of money either. We just lived frugal lives, spent our money, and hoped for the best.

I feel a lot of compassion for myself when I look back at those days. I really believed deep down that I wasn't worth earning a good income. A lot of my concerns had to do with my own lack of self-worth and how I questioned my abilities. That way of thinking can continue for years, and it will affect your income potential in a very deep way.

Unfortunately, those limiting beliefs can also prevent you from really enjoying money, even when you have it. You may think that you've overcome your issues by attracting more money into your life, but then you learn that you still struggle with your cash flow. When I was closing clients for my Facebook ads agency, I still did not make enough money to support myself because I kept hiring expensive contractors. In my mind, I still limited myself to earning $40,000 per year. While I brought in six-figures for my gross income, I did not believe that I deserved to be paid generously out of that amount.

Examining these beliefs surrounding money is essential, especially before you make sales calls and state your pricing to prospective clients. These beliefs will seep into your sales process, poisoning the waters. If you feel as though you are not worth much and that you don't deserve to earn a good income, you will either price yourself too low or let people bully you with their demands for a discount. You will have a harder time saying no to people who are not a good fit for you because deep down inside you think you don't deserve better.

Many of us believe that we are just not deserving enough, and when you proceed from that place, then abundance is a foreign concept. You've probably heard the term "scarcity mindset." This thought process is what breeds an attitude of competition because you think that there are limited resources and only a few "worthy" people who deserve to receive them.

I read a lot of books that were very useful in helping me overcome my internal money issues. I've discovered that positive affirmations by themselves don't really work. But looking at old beliefs with the help of a professional and learning to let go of some of the shame, blame, and pain of childhood memories related to money is very helpful.

Money is energy. Money is a friend. Money is meant to come into your possession so that you can benefit yourself and others. Money is not dirty or evil. It will only amplify the qualities of the person who uses it. So, if you're naturally a person with misguided intentions, having a lot of wealth will amplify those evil attributes. Many women make the mistake of believing that people who have a lot of money are not ethical people, and therefore, they suppress the desire to earn an abundant income. They don't want to be seen as corrupt, but this belief is faulty thinking.

I think that a successful person can have both an abundant financial lifestyle, as well as lead her life as a generous member of society. Prosperous people can treat themselves to massages and nice vacations while giving to a charity for sexual abuse survivors. Wealth doesn't have to automatically equal corruption. In fact, money makes the world function and it can be used for noble causes. But money can also be used for simple, frivolous things. Sometimes I like to take myself out to a nice vegetarian sushi meal and then buy a pair of earrings for myself as a treat. Just because I earn money doesn't mean that I have to give everything away to charity. There's a balance.

You do beneficial work in the world and you deserve to be paid well for what you do. You contribute to the well-being of other people and help their businesses thrive. Your impact is meaningful and important, therefore, there's no shame in getting paid what you are worth. But if you don't go through the laundry list of ways that you hold yourself back from receiving the abundance which is all around you, you'll always suffer when it comes to money. You won't have enough because you'll always think that you're not enough.

I feel a lot of sadness when I see women putting themselves down because I can see their true worth and what they are capable of bringing out to the world. I used to belittle myself as well. Some of my deeply ingrained beliefs really made no logical sense.

My dad was the breadwinner of the house when I was younger. He worked as an electrical engineer and made six figures a year. I came to believe that as a woman, I could never make as much as he did. On one hand, I thought that I needed a master's or doctorate degree to achieve that wealth. But on the other hand, I couldn't imagine myself happy or making good money in a profession I loved. My dad really enjoyed his work and took a lot of pride in it. I really didn't believe I was smart enough to pull that off too.

What limiting beliefs hold you back from a life of abundance, love, and success? Do you think that if you earn money, you can't be happy in the world simultaneously? Do you secretly believe that you don't deserve to be paid as well as men? Did you grow up in a household where your parents fought about money? Was money a dirty or unspoken subject to talk about? Do you currently fight about money with your partner? Do you think that only dishonest or immoral people make it to the top?

When you start to get clear on what you believe about money, you can slowly start to change these beliefs by instilling new ones into your mind. I use new money affirmations and statements in order to make these changes in my own life. One of my previous beliefs about money is that women were not capable of earning a decent paycheck. I have since turned this belief around into the statement: "Women have a capacity to earn an abundant living using their skills, talents, and expertise."

Once you recognize your worth, you will set your prices to reflect that worth and confidently state those prices during your sales calls. You won't let your old beliefs dominate you or dictate what you participate in. When you let go of these beliefs, you also attract new people to support this type of internal growth.

### *Your Turn: Changing Your Limiting Money Beliefs*

*The following is a common exercise that I've learned from other money-mindset professionals. Take out your journal and make two columns. In the first column, write down all the negative statements you heard about money when you were growing up, or even in adulthood. Some common ones are, "Money doesn't grow on trees," or "Money is the root of all evil."*

*Then, in the second column, write statements that actually counteract the first list or expand upon the old belief to make them more positive. For example, when you write,*

*"Money is the root of all evil," in the left column, you can explain in the right column the following rebuttal: "Money is misused by evil people but many good people do impactful actions with money."*

*Read aloud the new statements on the right-hand side of your list and practice your new affirmations on a daily basis. Reinforce these useful statements as your new beliefs and remove the negative connotations of money.*

# Week 3

# Day 11: Underpricing and Overpricing

Now that you've got your mindset in order and you have a good daily mindset routine, the next step in your sales process is to evaluate your pricing. When you're first starting out, it's quite common to logically tell yourself that you should price yourself lower than your competitors.

Often times you need to gain more experience to build your confidence and social proof. When I first started out doing social media marketing, I charged $300 per month for my first package, a price much lower than my competitors. That roughly came out to $50 per hour. For someone who had been in the nonprofit world for previous seven years making $20 per hour, I thought this price was great!

Other people offer their services for free in exchange for testimonials when they are just starting out. I think that trade is perfectly fine because once again, you're going to gain momentum by actually gaining experience from a project. And once you have one project under your belt, it's so much easier to talk about your experience on a sales call and confidently show people what you've done, even if it was just working with one other client for free or a nominal fee.

What I often see people do is stay at that low, initial price for a very long time - several years into their business, in fact. Many women that I coach keep their prices low for multiple reasons. They think that they are not worth charging more. Their clients may get really amazing results, but the women still tend not to give themselves enough credit for facilitating those transformations.

The other reason I see businesswomen undercharging is that they feel sympathetic toward their prospective clients who are struggling financially or emotionally, and they really want to help those people. However, they don't see that by undercharging they are actually doing themselves a disservice in that moment.

I also want to help as many people as possible, but what I learned through my years of being a business owner is that, A) You're not going to be able to help everyone, and B) You have to take care of yourself before you can take care of others. I had a tendency to want to give myself away in order to feel good about myself. At one point, I paid my contractors large sums of money but barely paid myself. I needed to learn how to value myself and believe that I was worthy of getting paid well.

If you are currently not making the type of money that you want, it is a great idea to start with examining your pricing. At what level do your competitors price themselves? Why do you feel as though you cannot charge this amount? How do you benefit by giving other people free or discounted services when you are not able to buy the items you need or your own family has to go without certain objects?

The other concern about underpricing yourself is that prospective clients won't take you seriously if you give your products and services away for such a low cost. They will think that your product is not worth their time or effort. The people who want a bargain and who shop around for the best price are usually the ones who are also going to be high-maintenance clients. They are often demanding and entitled when it comes to your services. A few high-paying clients with whom you can give your full attention are far more preferable than many lower paying clients who need a ton of attention.

Some women entrepreneurs also go to the extreme end and offer their services for either free or for trade. I think if you're starting out, offering your service once or twice for free in exchange for testimonials can help build credibility and confidence. However, if you consistently offer to do something for free, you're not valuing yourself in the long run. The same lesson goes for bartering. I am very selective with who I do trades with now. I only barter for services I really want, such as a massage. If you trade your time too often for free, it will be difficult to create time for paying clients.

Here's the flipside to pricing yourself too low - overpricing. This issue is the other mistake which I see a lot of new women entrepreneurs make, especially ones who have taken expensive online coaching programs. Many of these programs advocate for entrepreneurs to raise their prices dramatically and suddenly. High-priced coaches call this upsell "premium pricing." They encourage their students to create some arbitrary "high-ticket offer" which costs $3k or more and to pitch it confidently in their sales calls.

I completely disagree with this way of thinking. If you've been charging $300 per month and you are suddenly encouraged to pitch a deal for $7,500, your inner self is not going to be able to catch up with your external self. You're going to experience some major cognitive dissonance. Even if you've been working on your mindset and your childhood beliefs around money, making a jump this dramatic is going to be difficult for many people.

What tends to happen to people when they make such a large jump in price is that they subconsciously still believe that they are not worthy of that price. From that belief system, they have a tendency to sabotage certain potential deals. I've seen some very confident people go through this process and claim high-priced deals that way. But I don't think it's the norm for everyone.

The best way to handle your pricing is to value your services "just right," at a price point reminiscent of what Goldilocks was going for! When you are not underpricing or overcharging, you will show up to your sales calls with self-assurance. You won't feel guilty for charging too much and you won't undervalue yourself. It will feel just right. This place is where the real confidence comes from. Plus, you won't feel bad saying no to people who aren't a good fit because you know what you're worth and you're willing to stick to that price.

If you've charged a lower sum for a long time, don't make the mistake of jacking up your prices arbitrarily. Try to build up your confidence in stages by increasing your prices gradually, in steps. If you have a client who was with you from the beginning and is getting a killer deal with your low initial price, try to first secure another client at your new rate before approaching your current one and telling them that your prices have gone up. You can explain the reason and that you haven't done a price increase in a while.

Then, if that client is not okay with the price increase, be prepared to let them go. You may be surprised that they accept your price increase gracefully, and perhaps they wondered for a while why you charged them so little for the amazing service you provided all along!

When you have a price that you can confidently tell people about, you don't have to be ashamed about what you offer or the price of your services. You can calmly segue into price during your sale, and it won't be a shock to either you or your prospective client.

## Your Turn: Pricing Yourself Right

*Think about your current pricing and answer the following questions in your journal:*

1. *What do your competitors charge for this same service? Do they have the same experience or do they get similar results for their clients as you do?*

2. *When was the last time that you raised your rates? What do you feel inside when you think about your current pricing?*

3. *Write down a number which you think is not too low or too high for your pricing. Say it out loud in a full sentence, as though you are telling a prospective client what your package or offer is worth. How does it feel?*

# Day 12: Creating Your Sales Script

Before I enrolled in an online coaching program, I never really had a structure or script for my sales calls. I just went with the flow of the conversation. I naturally started with a little bit of small talk with the prospective client and then transitioned into talking about their business. The calls were very random, to be honest.

When I first started out with my business, I also wasted a lot of time meeting people face-to-face in coffee shops. I've learned over time that this is not the best plan because sometimes you meet with someone and know within a few minutes that they are not a good fit for you. You might quickly learn that they are actually part of a multi-level marketing scheme and they only pretended to be interested in your service so they could peddle their strange products! Then you have to gently find a way to say no to them while not be irritated for taking two hours out of your day.

When you start your sales conversation with people, you really need to have a solid plan and structure. This system will help you if you are typically nervous on your sales calls and feel as though you freeze up when you are in front of a prospective client. If you have the structure memorized internally, then you can relax more and not have to worry about what you will say next. I don't recommend that you read your script word for word because you will sound very robotic and unnatural. You will have a hard time genuinely connecting to the person in front of you and listening closely to them if you are focused on a written script.

Here's the general structure of my sales calls:

1. Building Rapport
2. Framing the Call
3. Asking the Right Questions
4. Reviewing the Budget
5. Transitioning to Your Offer
6. Asking for the Sale
7. Answering Questions / Overcoming Objections
8. Reviewing the Next Steps

I will cover each one of these eight sections in more detail, but I wanted you to see the basic flow of the conversation. You will find that one section easily flows into the next section. When you're creating your own sales script with this framework in mind, you will just jot down notes and ideas which prompt you to say what you need to say next.

Remember that you are the one they contacted which means you naturally get to be the leader of this conversation. If you remember to think of this exchange as a "service call" rather than a "sales call," you can relax even more. You give them as much value as you can on the call and help them out, even if you don't make the sale. I give people resources and referrals all the time, especially once I figure out that I can't help them personally.

Essentially, you try to ascertain exactly what this person's problem really is, whether or not you can help fix that problem, and whether or not this person is a good fit for your business. Your script will help you determine whether the prospective client has the same values as you, fits the characteristics which you listed in your ideal customer profile, and does not try to negotiate too far down with your price point.

By internalizing your sales script and going through this process, you will be able to identify the types of clients you know you can serve. You don't want to read this script word for word. In essence, you want this to be your guide for how you structure your overall interactions with prospective clients. A script will help you formulate a way to relate to them and guide them to the decision of wanting to work with you.

### Your Turn: Creating Your Sales Script

*Journal about how you feel using a sales script. Do you feel like it would help your sales process or hinder your spontaneity? Why or why not?*

# Day 13: Building Rapport

Now that you know the background on why it's important to have a sales script, let's talk about building rapport with your prospective client. Building rapport is just a fancy term for connecting with your prospective client in a friendly, warm way. You never want to jump right into a business conversation if you can help it. Some people are extremely business-oriented and will really want to cut to the chase with you. If that's the case, you can mirror those clients and get right down to business. Ask them about how they got started with the business, which is always a good opening topic.

But for the most part, you need to create a connection with your prospective client by chatting about mundane things. Where are they from? What do they like to do there? How was their weekend? How is the weather? Taking a few minutes at the opening to have a friendly, warm, casual conversation will also ease any tension or fear you may have, and many people appreciate this dialogue.

Overall, when I build rapport with someone, I ask them questions and listen to their answers. I also share small pieces of information about myself. I tell people on the phone that I live in Northern California and that it's only 25 minutes from the ocean. Then I might make a small comment about how cold the Pacific Ocean is. You shouldn't spend a ton of time going on and on about yourself, but by sharing small tidbits of information, you foster a connection with the other person.

If you're not a natural at building rapport, that's totally fine. Write down some standard go-to questions that you can easily rely upon and practice them with friends and colleagues. You can also practice them in real life by going to networking meetings and make it a goal to talk to a certain number of strangers during those meetings.

### *Your Turn: Learning to Build Rapport*

*Write out your list of go-to rapport building questions which you can always have handy for your script. Ask ones which feel natural to you. Practice them in front of a mirror or role play with a friend.*

*Here's a few examples to get you started:*

1. *I see you are in the (xxx) area code. Where is that exactly?*
2. *What are the best things to do in that area?*
3. *How did you end up there?*
4. *I noticed in your "About" section on your website that you enjoy _____ (whatever they mentioned). How did you get into that?*

***Bonus Exercise:*** *Make a date in your calendar to go to a networking event and practice* your questions *in real life with at least three people whom you have never met before!*

# Day 14: Framing the Call

After you've built rapport with your prospective client, make a smooth transition by framing the call and setting up expectations. This frame is a very brief part of your script that you will eventually memorize so that it doesn't sound unnatural or forced. Remember that the prospective client is on the phone with you for a reason.

They have either seen your ad, met you at a networking meeting, noticed your content on social media, or found something appealing about you. You are the person who could potentially solve their problem, the one with the answers for them. It also means that you are the one who guides the call.

Framing the call not only helps set the right expectations, but it also puts you in the driver's seat. It will help remind you that you are the one setting the whole tone for the call and you are interviewing the prospective clients as much as they are interviewing you. If you can remember those points, then you're going to be fine. You don't have to worry as much about the outcome of the call. You can just be your authentic self.

I usually start framing the call by mentioning how much time the call will take and that I will ask the prospective clients certain questions related to their business. Because I have often done sales for digital marketing agencies, I tell the prospective client that I will go over questions related to what they have done in the past about their marketing, as well as other nuts and bolts of their business, and their goals. If I think that we may be a good fit to work together,

I explain the next steps to them. Then I ask them, "How does that sound?"

I wait for them to agree before I move forward with the call. I really want to know that we are all on the same page. I also tell them that the call is being recorded for training purposes, but only if that's the case. When I have the green light from them, I can move on to transitioning into the next step to ask guided questions about any issues in their business.

### *Your Turn: How to Frame Your Call*

*Take a moment to write out in your journal your word-for-word script for framing the call. Here's my example which you can use as a reference:*

*"Thanks again (Prospective Client) for booking a call with me today. I'm excited to learn more about your business. Today we're going to take 30-minutes to go over your situation. I will ask you questions related to your business or circumstance, your previous marketing, and what your goals are. At the end, if I think that we may be a good fit to work together, I will share with you my pricing and the next steps. Even if we don't end up working together, I will still give you some strategy advice and tips which you can start to apply immediately to your situation. How does that sound?"*

- *Once you have a script that you like, start practicing it out loud. The more you practice your script, the more it will sound natural during your actual call.*

# Day 15: Asking Guiding Questions

In this component of your call, you will ask the prospective clients powerful questions which get them to think very deeply about their business or life. This section is where you dig deep to delve into their "pain points." You've probably heard this term before. Essentially, you try to figure out the biggest issue, get the prospective clients to recognize that issue, and then summarize it for them so that the issue is something that they really can't deny. Creating a sense of urgency around solving this problem, so that you can then position yourself as the answer to their need, is also important.

You don't necessarily want to jump right into the point of their pain directly. Start by asking them questions which will give you a sense of:

1. What has happened in the past?

2. What is their current situation?

3. Where do they want to go (i.e., what are their goals)?

Let's imagine that you are a fitness coach, for example. Knowing what types of fitness plans they have tried to follow in the past is going to be very helpful information for you. Have they worked with other personal trainers before? If so, how did that go? What was challenging about their exercise plans in the past?

For the next step, you might ask them about their present situation. What are they currently doing with their exercise and eating habits? Do they have trouble sleeping? Are they experiencing any pain or symptoms in their body? What types of exercise and activities do they love doing and which ones do they dread?

Lastly, you want to pinpoint their future goals. What are their ideal weight goals? Where do they see themselves in six months? What would make them feel proud? It's important to spend a significant amount of time on their goals to start painting the portrait of how it would feel to meet those goals. This feeling is what you're really going after. People buy on emotion and they actually look to purchase the feeling of the result.

For example, if you ask them, "What would it do for you if you lost 20 pounds, and how would that make you feel?" then you give them the opportunity to daydream about what it would actually look like to reach those goals. You will help them see what's possible by planting this significant question in your script.

Within those questions, you want to peel away the surface and get to the heart of their issues. For example, if someone is looking for a fitness coach, the real reason that they may want to work out more often is perhaps that they want more energy to be able to play with their kids or to feel a sense of enthusiasm and joy for their life. Pay particular attention to these deeper insights and write them down because you will refer back to them and summarize them when you pitch the price for your services.

The questions you ask should definitely be related to your particular industry, but there's also a general sense of digging into the heart of a prospective client's problem and unearthing the core essence of that person and their ultimate issue. Your job is to be a detective, trying to find this central truth by asking the right questions and helping them understand their situation now, as well as where they want to go.

### *Your Turn: Creating Your List of Guiding Questions*

*List 12 to 15 sales questions you think are relevant to your particular industry. Bundle them into lists of easy, medium, and hard, including four or five questions in each section. Once you have your questions, ask them out loud and imagine your prospective clients answering them. Which ones do you think will lead your client to think more about their struggle and their situation? Here are a few examples of questions you can consider:*

1. *How did you get into your business? (for business to business clients)*

2. *What have you been struggling with the most recently?*

3. *What have you done to address these issues so far?*

4. *If you could resolve this problem, what would that do for your life?*

# Week 4

# Day 16: Reviewing the Budget

It's important in the first conversation that you deal directly with questions related to budget because it will get the prospective client thinking about money in general. If you're able to get a sense of what they are willing to spend, you will be able to see if they are a good fit for you. For example, if you sell a $3k package and the clients say that they budgeted only $500 for this type of service, you have a real problem.

Most of the time, you'll find that people say that they don't know what their budget is. I try to probe them a bit deeper and put out a higher number in order to see what their reaction is. If you put out a higher number at first, then they won't be as shocked about your own prices later on.

I found that many prospects do have an idea of what they ideally want to spend and they are shopping around to find the best deal. They may not want to tell you outright what their ideal budget is because they want you to give an indication of your prices first so that they can compare your cost with another company's offerings.

As a consumer, I can empathize with people who want to save money, but a prospective client could potentially be a headache for you if they attempt to get a bargain. For one thing, they may not fully value what you have to offer or they may have unrealistic expectations going into the working relationship.

If the prospective client has worked with another business similar to yours, it's wise to ask them what they are currently spending on that provider. Once again, they may not want to be upfront about that expense because they first wish to compare what you will provide them. But it does not hurt to ask. This information will give you insights about their overall expectations.

Sometimes the prospects will ask your opinion on how much you think they should spend on their particular need. They may be gauging your prices at that point and would like more information on what you exactly provide. It's up to you whether or not you would like to give a range of your pricing at this point or whether you think it's better to turn the question back to them.

If someone absolutely refuses to talk about their budget, make a note of it and move on. Sometimes it's a red flag, but sometimes they genuinely don't know because someone else on their team is in charge of budget matters.

Overall, if the prospective client doesn't answer your questions in general or gives you one-word answers, this should signify a red flag in the conversation. You want to see what this person would be like to work with in the long run, and you don't want to onboard anyone with whom you see potential problems, especially in communicating.

So, don't be shy in asking about their budget directly. This conversation will also give you an opportunity to tell them if their budget expectations are realistic in the particular industry that you are in. This way, you prime them for having an honest conversation about your pricing, and there will be no surprises.

### *Your Turn: Forming the Best Budget Questions*

*Write out the exact question of how you want to
ask potential clients about their budget. For example, you
can simply say, "What do you expect to pay for a program
which will help you reach those goals you mentioned?"
Write out a response to their potential "I don't know"
answer. Practice this response out loud until it becomes
natural.*

# Day 17: Transitioning to Your Offer

Once you ask your prospective client the right questions about their previous situations and their goals, you will want to find an elegant way to transition to their offer. Sometimes it's helpful to summarize the main "pain points" of their personal struggles and the goals which they want to achieve. Here's an example:

*"Ms. Prospective Client, thank you so much for sharing this information with me today. It's been very helpful for me to learn about your journey so far. You mentioned that you've struggled in your business to get enough leads and previously have relied upon word-of-mouth referrals. Sometimes you will only get three new leads per month, and that puts a lot of pressure on you to close them.*

*You brought up that you have a hard time marketing yourself online and you feel really confused about all the different ways of doing it. You also don't have the time or desire to learn it on your own. You would like to build your business to $20k per month because that will give you more freedom to be with your husband and your two children, but you also want to spend some creative time designing new products. Did you want to add anything else to this summary?"*

If you really listened to the prospective client and have taken good notes, this part should be easy to recount to the client. After the client has soaked in their situation (and are internally impressed that you remembered so much about what they said), then you can transition into your offer. I personally like to add a segueing statement, asking the prospective client if they have any questions before I go into my offer. This works pretty well and gives you an opportunity to move into your pricing smoothly.

Remember that you have the power over whether or not you want to pitch to a prospective client. If you don't think they are a good fit, be upfront with them instead of desperately pitching your offer and then hoping for the best. You deserve to work with clients who are committed, communicate well, and happily accept your pricing.

When I trained to do sales calls for digital-marketing agencies, we often did a two-call process, where the first call was devoted only to asking poignant and significant questions and the second call was for actually pitching the price to the client. We were told to either give a range for the services if they asked or to say something like, "I don't know exactly what the price will be until the team reviews your information."

We avoided naming a specific cost for a couple reasons. First, we didn't want to shock the prospective client with the price because were selling high-ticket items. I pitched set-up fees from $5,000 to $10,000 or more. Secondly, we wanted to separate the "service call" from the "sales call," so that we could play the investigator and valuable contributor role as much as possible on that first call. That way, we could just be present with the other person on the line and not worry about closing the sale.

Most likely, you'll do a one-call close for your service. Technically, you will probably need to make a couple of follow-up calls until you close the deal. Many people say they need to "think about it," and there could be some hidden objections or reluctance which you will need to uncover. I will address this issue a bit later.

### *Your Turn: Finding a Transition Phrase*

*Write in your journal the exact phrase you would like to use when you transition from asking your questions to actually introducing your offer. Read it to yourself first and then read it out loud. How does your voice sound? Does it sound natural or forced?*

*The second step to write down is a short script on how to gently tell someone that they are not a good fit for you at this time. Explain in a clear and honest way why you think that you both would not benefit from working together - whether it is price or some other reason.*

*Remember that you can always offer the prospective client resources or referrals which may benefit them. You're not losing a potential client; you are opening the door for your ideal client to sign up with you.*

# Day 18: Pitching and Asking for the Sale

Many of my clients get nervous around the part of sale when they have to ask for money. They have a difficult time transitioning from helping people to actually approaching the prospective client with their offer and saying exactly how much it will cost. I used to struggle with these issues in my mind as well. These concerns had to do with one or more of these three items:

1. I didn't feel worthy.

2. I was afraid I would get rejected by the client.

3. Someone told me I should charge a certain amount, but deep down it didn't feel right.

4. The sale felt invasive or rude because I never talked openly about money when I grew up.

Let me address each of these items one-by-one.

**"I didn't feel worthy."** I talked about this topic previously in the section on mindset, but it's an important one to revisit again. If you don't feel worthy, you're not going to be able to confidently pitch your price and ask for the sale. It's going to feel awkward and uncomfortable.

Yes, you are worthy of being paid for your services, even if you are in a helping profession. You provide massive value for that person and help them solve problems which they could not solve on their own. You transform their lives. And it's okay to be paid for that! There's no inner conflict that you need to solve.

**"I was afraid I would get rejected by the client."** Actually, getting rejected by the client isn't necessarily a serious setback. It just means that this particular person is not a good fit for your business, or is afraid of committing to themselves and the process. When a person says no to me, I don't take it personally anymore. If they are not ready to be helped, I won't be able to get them the results they are looking for anyway.

If I tell them my price and they scoff at it or ask who I think I am for charging that amount, I can calmly maintain my professionalism and tell them why I charge what I do. I know that I'm worth the investment because I've consciously not overpriced or underpriced my work. It's just right. People who shop around for the lowest deal are not going to be your ideal clients anyway.

**"Someone told me I should charge a certain amount, but deep down it didn't feel right."** I used to dread the part of the sales call when I had to talk about my price because an online coach told me that I needed to pitch $10k deals to be profitable with the costs of my team. That was back when I was chasing the $100k per month dream that wasn't really mine.

There is definitely logic in protecting your profit margins. When you just start out, you need to validate in your own mind that you can really help someone and produce the desired results. You have to work within your own comfort zone while also challenging yourself to grow and stretch to overcome your fears.

**"The sale felt invasive or rude because I never talked openly about money when I grew up."** Listen, most of us did not grow up in an environment where it was encouraged to openly discuss money or have a healthy relationship with it. You most likely have had to deal with overcoming some negative or limiting beliefs surrounding money, your value, and pricing. Give yourself a break.

What do you do to overcome these fears? Build what you need to say into a sales script and follow the formula.

The best formula I have found is to summarize the main pain points of the prospective client's concerns, emphasizing how they currently feel and where exactly the struggle lies. Then you pave the way for a different future and how it would feel to reach their goals. If you pitch a high-ticket item and are a B2B service provider, you should couch the deal in terms of what types of financial goals can be reached within the next 12 months.

For example, if the prospective client wants to earn $20,000 per month, you can say, "You mentioned to me that your goal was to reach $20,000 per month or $240,000 per year. To get started with our program, it is only $5000." The purpose of framing your pitch this way is that the investment seems miniscule compared to the potential profit gain.

If you are a business-to-consumer provider, like a therapist or life coach, you should summarize what the person told you in terms of their goals before pitching your price. This reminder ultimately expresses to them the value they will receive. You might say, "You mentioned to me that one of your goals is to lose 20 pounds and exercise three times a week so that you can have more energy to play with your kids. To achieve those goals in my fitness program, the cost is $2,000 for 3 months."

Once you've pitched your price, it's essential that you don't say anything afterwards! This pause will feel incredibly uncomfortable and you may internally want to break that silence, but don't be tempted to do it. Negotiation studies show that the person who speaks first is more likely to concede. That means you have to show some discipline in that moment after your pitch and hold your ground. Some people like to put themselves on mute at this crucial moment in order to not be tempted, but do whatever works for you.

The goal is to eventually get to a point where you are not as nervous talking about the price. Just make it a very casual, matter-of-fact part of the conversation. This moment of calm goes back to your mindset. If you begin to make a big deal about the price, your prospective client will follow your lead and start to get worried about the price as well. The client feeds off your energy.

You will most likely get some follow-up questions or objections after you mention your price, but I will teach you how to address these in the next section. If you don't really have much more to say to the person, it's essential to ask for the sale at this point in the conversation. Many people forget this part. Ask to get their credit card number to take a deposit or the full payment right then and there. Don't give people an opportunity to mull it over several days or shop around. If you did your sales process right, you will have already addressed those fears!

### *Your Turn: Creating Your Pitch*

*When you create your own pitch, you want to make it as simple as possible. One mistake many women make is talking too much during the pricing part and then nervously trying to justifying why they are worthy of the price they set. That's why it's useful to find wording which is straight and to the point.*

*Play around with wording which feels the most natural to you. You can use my example as a starting point to see what language feels right:*

*"You mentioned to me that your goal was to reach $20,000 per month or $240,000 per year. To get started with our program, it is only $5000."*

*Write down your own pitch, and then with a partner, practice being silent after your pitch. Tell them to pause for a few potent seconds before they answer so that you can practice being okay with that awkward silence. Over time, it won't feel as awkward!*

# Day 19: Answering Questions / Overcoming Objections

Once you pitch your price and are silent, the first words out of your prospective client's mouth will most likely be a question or an objection. These contentions don't necessarily mean that the person is not interested in your product or service or that they will refuse you right away. Sure, there will be some people who will think that your offer is way too expensive for them at the time and sometimes they will tell you that. But most people will probe you for a little more information on your offer or try to deflect going through the actual purchase cycle because they are uncomfortable with saying no.

When they ask you questions that are not automatically related to your price, it often means that you did a great job with the initial part of your sales call. You helped them to identify their main issue and envision a different future where you guide them to reach their goals. In other words, they may see the value of your product or service, and potentially they want to find a way to make it work for them.

But, a series of questions could also mean that they are shopping around and asking each of the potential providers specific questions to compare with others. No matter the reason, you should always try to answer each question thoughtfully and concisely without rambling on or trying to justify yourself or the price. Many people, including myself make this mistake in their initial sales calls. When you try out a higher price for your services, sometimes you feel compelled to explain the new price. It is typical to want to justify yourself.

Be sure to write out a list of common questions and complaints, then answer them in the way that you think best explains your point of view, but also acknowledges the client's concerns. Telling the prospective client, "That's a great question," is very affirming. You can also make a comment using the feel-felt-found formula where you acknowledge the prospective client's feelings, say how other clients were in the exact same situation, and then explain how your clients found that you provided them a certain solution. Here's an example:

*"I know it's a lot of money to invest upfront and it can feel scary. Many of our clients initially felt the same way. But they have found that the return on their investment made the expenditure worthwhile in the end because they discovered more freedom to be creative in their business while their marketing was taken care of."*

The more prepared you are with solid answers for these questions, the more confident you will be in handling the objections. Don't take the questions personally. See them as a small challenge in getting to your goal of signing someone up. You can also take moments in your answers to put in mini-case studies and wins for your own clients in order to build your credibility or explain something in an educational way.

I once pitched a $10k deal to one of the prospective clients of an agency I did sales for, and I could tell that they had their hesitations about moving forward with us. Sometimes it takes extra care and attention to ask the right questions and probe a little deeper to uncover the real reason behind someone's hesitation. I learned from them that out of 15 agencies, we were one of two which they were considering hiring. However, our fees were significantly higher.

I acknowledged and explained to the prospective client that we were definitely not the cheapest agency out there. But if they chose to go with an agency that charged less but couldn't produce the results, they would actually waste more time and money down the road. Also, I learned some valuable information from them. The other agency had offered a paid audit which was less of a risk for the client's company to take on. I instantly offered them our paid audit offer which showed them what our business was capable of. He pulled out his credit card on the spot. We ended up closing the deal and they paid upfront for a year.

This one little act of listening closely and then easing their minds in the objection phase led to closing the sale.

### *Your Turn: Preparing for Questions and Objections*

*Write out a list of five to ten common questions and objections to your offer, as well as the best answers. For example, a common objection might be that the prospective client feels the need to check in with his or her spouse before making a decision. Your response could be something like this:*

*"Absolutely! I always check with my significant other before making a big purchase as well. What types of questions do you think your spouse would have about my program and when do you plan on speaking to them?"*

*Practice these answers out loud until they become second nature for you. Find a partner to practice with as well, and get their feedback on how the answers sound. Ideally, practicing with someone you trust, who also happens to be in the category of your ideal client, is the best option! You want your answers to sound realistic, confident, and self-assured.*

# Day 20: Reviewing Next Steps with the Prospective Client

You've reached the final section of creating your sales script. That's reason to celebrate! You've also come to a crucial step in the sales-call process. This is when many people get tripped up because they are worried that they are going to appear too pushy, sales-y, or desperate. There's a way, however, to talk about the next steps with the clients and lay out the groundwork for following up with them without being too demanding.

One of my sales coaches told me to always assume the sale. That means you guide the prospective client to the end goal, educating them in a way that transitions into your onboarding process seamlessly and effortlessly. Assuming the sale doesn't mean that you're going to close everyone. That's impossible and quite unrealistic. Some people are naturally not going to be a good fit for you.

However, closing the deal has a great deal to do with your mindset. After you call someone and answer all their questions and objections as best as you can, you have two choices. Either you tell yourself you messed up, you believe that you suck at sales, and then you proceed to pick apart your call and harshly criticize everything you did, or you tell yourself that you did the best that you could, assume the sale, and then follow up with that prospective client.

After all the questions have been answered on the call, I like to go through the next steps of what the client can expect when working with me. This action is a description of your onboarding process which explains in detail what happens when they give you the green light. The client will most likely put their deposit or payment down, sign a contract, and then either fill out a more comprehensive questionnaire or set up an initial call with you. I always recommend taking a part of the payment if not the whole amount before you get started working with them. This down-payment will deter any clients from not paying you for your services!

You can transition into this final phase of the sales process in a very effortless way by simply saying, "Do you have any final questions before I describe some of our next steps?"

After you explain the next steps, the most important detail to complete is to ask the prospective client to describe how they feel so far. I use this technique to gauge their initial thoughts and try to reveal any hidden questions or concerns. I sometimes will ask them straight out if this deal was in alignment with their expectations or how we compare to our competitors. There's no need to feel shy about this question. Remember, you are still trying to figure out if you are a good fit to work together! Honesty and open communication are important qualities in any business dealings.

I don't pressure people to make a decision right then and there, the way some salespeople do. Instead, I prefer to give them a few days to do their research, mull the deal over, and talk to their coaches and/or spouses, if needed. Most likely, you won't get a straight, "Yes" (although those are always exciting!). It's even nice to get an immediate, "No," because then you know where they stand. I personally am not a fan of, "I need to think about it," because this phrase can actually mean a few other things.

1.  They actually need some time to think because they want to weigh all the information they've received and make sure that they make a sound business/life decision.

2.  They have hidden concerns they are not sharing with you.

3.  They are using that phrase as a polite "no."

Do the best you can to get to the heart of their concerns if you detect something is up. Use your instincts and ability to ask potent questions. You'll prevent potential "ghosting" situations where the client fails to return your calls or emails even though they may have initially expressed interest.

I typically ask to follow up with them via a scheduled phone call within two business days. This gives them enough time to "think about it," but also allows them to have a solid answer for you in a decent time frame. Avoid scheduling your follow-up call for longer than that time period because the prospective client will get distracted, have the opportunity to shop around to only get the best deal possible, or forget about the urgency behind their need.

Prospective clients are overwhelmed with all the choices that are available to them and it's important to capture their attention! Book the follow-up call for two business days out and send them an invite to that meeting so that they can add it to their calendar. Send them a follow-up email to say that you enjoyed speaking with them and confirm the date and time of the follow up. You can also include links to case studies or testimonials concerning your services in that email.

Here's a sample of a follow up email I've sent out:

*Hi Prospective Client,*

*It was wonderful speaking with you just now.*

*Thanks for taking the time to share details of your business and current Facebook ad situation.*

*Here is the link to the testimonials and case studies I mentioned.*

*I sent you an invite for our follow-up call on Friday, January 18th at 10:00 am PST.*

*Please let me know if you have any questions and have a great rest of your day!*

*Jula*

If the prospective client does not want to book a follow-up call with you, ask them if you can email them to check in on a particular date. This step is important because you can make a note in your CRM when to follow up with that person, and they will expect your email if you don't hear from them first.

### *Your Turn: Reviewing the Next Steps*

*A. Write out a short paragraph describing the next steps of your onboarding process. Answer the following questions to help you create your response:*

*1. Do you accept deposits? If so, when is the full amount due?*

*2. Do you send out a briefing document or questionnaire?*

*3. Do you have an initial kick-off call? If so, what does that entail?*

*4. Is there a hand-off with another team member? When will this occur?*

*5. How often will you communicate with them in the first few weeks?*

*6. Is there a set-up period? If so, how long will that last?*

*7. Do they get reports, check-ins, reviews, or monthly calls?*

*After you have completed this paragraph, be sure to practice it out loud to internalize this part of your script.*

*B. Create a follow-up email template for you to send out which already has links to case-studies and testimonials, if you have them. Review the example I gave in this section as a reference.*

# <u>Week 5</u>

# Day 21: Practicing Your Script

Let's review the structure of your script and put it all together:

1. Building Rapport
2. Framing the Call
3. Asking the Right Questions
4. Reviewing the Budget
5. Transitioning to Your Offer
6. Asking for the Sale
7. Answering Questions / Overcoming Objections
8. Reviewing the Next Steps

After doing each of the previous exercises, you should have a comprehensive script to start practicing from.

They say that practice makes perfect, and I couldn't agree more. If you're a beginner to sales, the first fifty calls that you do with clients may feel a bit awkward and uncomfortable because you're not used to them. You may feel your heart pounding in your chest when you pitch your price. You may stumble around for things to say during the rapport-building segment. Or you may just be at a loss of words when someone comes out with a strong objection.

That's completely okay because I once felt this way too!

Selling is a skill that you can learn and you must remember that. Do you think that an accomplished professional pianist played difficult pieces with perfection the first time they ever laid their fingers on piano keys? No way! It's okay to stumble around in the beginning of your sales calls because you're learning how to internalize your script and to use the best choice of words in any given moment. You're learning how to be natural while practicing being of service to another person, yet still assertively transitioning to the sale.

So, the moral of the story is practice, practice, practice. Practice with a role-play partner. Practice by yourself. Practice in the mirror. Practice to your dog. Just do it! The more often you hear yourself say the words out loud, the better. You will become more comfortable with your script, and eventually it will become a part of you, rather than an awkward, foreign system that you have to learn and follow. You will be able to improvise on the spot once you get a foundation in place.

When I was first learning sales, I actually called one of my fellow students and had him pretend to be a prospective client. We went through the whole sales script that way. Having someone else on another phone was really good for me because it made the situation feel more real. You can try this with a willing friend as well, especially if they fit the profile of your ideal client. That way, they can answer your questions in a genuine way. Who knows? They may even want to become your real client!

The goal of practicing your script is to internalize it as much as you can. Chances are, you're going to sound a bit unsure of yourself in the beginning. But if you have the structure of your script inside you and if you have repeated it over and over again, you'll have more room to relax and to be spontaneous as well.

Don't worry about whether you follow the script perfectly. It's best to have the structure memorized as much as possible so that you can observe its flow naturally, but if you miss a few sections, don't panic. You obviously don't want to sound as though you are reading a script word for word. You can use your script as a general guide during your calls and a reference if you need to jog your memory.

I am not sure why many people think that they can just "wing it" on their sales calls. Because sales is a learnable skill, like any other skill, you have to put the time in. Just like with exercising, some days you'll feel like it; some days you won't. But if you can make this commitment to yourself, then you'll improve every single day.

Set aside a certain amount of time each day for your practice sessions. I actually put tasks like that in my calendar in order to hold myself accountable, and I treat those sessions just like an appointment or an actual sales call. You can also trick yourself by saying that you'll practice for five minutes. You'll probably be surprised when you see that 20 or 30 minutes have whizzed by.

Russell Brunson, the owner of Clickfunnels, said that the first 40 episodes of his podcast weren't that great because he was just starting to get the hang of it. He was beginning to find his voice but he didn't give up. Now he can go onto a stage in front of thousands of people because he's gotten to the point where all of his repeated stories have been internalized.

When you practice, you also give yourself permission to make mistakes, to stumble a bit on your pitch, to feel the discomfort of saying the new price out loud. When you breathe through these issues and work at them every day, you'll see the improvements and can celebrate these small wins in yourself.

### *Your Turn: Practicing with a Friend*

*Ask a friend to play your prospective client in an actual phone call. Run through the whole script with them and ask them to throw out a few common objections which you hear often related to pricing, needing to "think about it," and so on. After the call, ask them for their honest feedback. Ask what you did really well and what you could have done differently. Write in your journal how it felt to do the exercise and what you learned.*

# Day 22: Recording Your Calls

I recommend recording all your calls and listening to them. I don't know many people who love hearing themselves on the other side of recordings. However, it's an extremely good discipline to start. I admit that I have a hard time listening to my own recordings too. I usually just have a vague feeling of how a call went. "Oh, that was a pretty decent call." But when you listen to how you actually sound, you will pick up on issues that you didn't even realize.

You may, for example, pick up on how many times you say the word "um" or another filler word like "totally." I used to have a business developer who often said the word "awesome" and she emphasized it for things that actually weren't that awesome, so it tended to sound a bit contrived overall. Pay attention to your tone of voice, your energy level, whether or not you sound as though you are following a script, etc.

Some other things to pay attention to during your recordings:

1. How you sound when you pitch your price. Are you confident or nervous?

2. What the subtle reactions are from your prospective client. Can you notice some clues on their excitement or enthusiasm? Do you sense hesitation or concern?

3. How you end the call. Do you mention that you are excited to work with them? It's similar to a job

interview when you show the interviewer how enthusiastic you would be to start the job.

4. How smoothly you answer questions or objections. Does it sound like you know what you are talking about? Can you confidently answer questions and do you show them your expertise?

5. How you manage the transitions in your calls and the overall flow. Are you guiding and leading the prospective client or are you often led or dominated by them?

Once again be gentle on yourself! Your first few recorded calls may feel a bit painful to listen to, but they contain valuable information for you to improve day by day.

Hiring a sales coach to listen to your calls and provide feedback may also be a useful experience. They will be able to pick up on certain concerns which you may miss when you listen to your own recordings. For example, a sales coach can analyze your tone of voice and hear speech patterns that you may not be aware of. You may need to tweak just one small thing with your pitch in order to close more prospective clients.

### Your Turn: Recording Your Calls

*Record one of your calls, whether a real-life one or a practice, and listen to yourself on the call. Pay attention to how you sound in the rapport-building section, with your transitions, in your actual pitch, and the follow up. Write in your journal at least three areas where you think you did well during the call and three items which you can improve upon.*

# Day 23: Note Taking and Tracking Your Clients

There are a few logistical items that I need to address with you. In sales, you are playing a numbers game. At the end of the day, you never know how many people are actually interested in moving forward with you and when you should follow up, unless you keep good notes and have a decent client relationship management (CRM) system. It pays to stay organized because if one prospective client expressed interest, but mentioned that she can only start after she receives her tax return, you want to mark the date of when to follow up with her.

I personally use a simple spreadsheet to write notes on how the calls went and to track information such as the client's phone number and email address so that I have a bird's eye overview of my monthly calls. Then I track my calls in my CRM along with my notes. However, a CRM is a great tool. Be sure to try out several and see which one suits your needs. The important point is that you take good notes during your actual sales call so that you can recall vital information in order to close the sale.

The notes that I take range from the personal, like where the prospective client lives and how many kids they have, to their pain points and frustrations about their business. Writing down information about their main issue is extremely important because then you can refer back to those pain points when you build your case on why they need assistance from you. Repeating back their own words to them is quite powerful because it helps the prospective client realize that they need you! They essentially sell to themselves.

If I am on a second call with a client, I read the notes back to them in a summary before I launch into that follow-up call. The prospective client will be impressed that you took good notes and really listened to them. You'll make an excellent impression. This summary will also help you refresh your own memory as well.

Think about the time you went to your dentist and six months later they were able to ask you about the European vacation that you took. How would they be able to remember such a personal detail? They did it by taking good notes! I bet that attention to detail made you feel warm and fuzzy inside, and you probably felt important for that one brief moment. People like to be heard and seen.

In regards to having a good tracking and note-taking system, it's also a good idea to have a consistent system where you can see how often you close with your prospective clients. When you know your closing rate, you can make adjustments accordingly.

With my simple spreadsheet for an overview, I can go in and see exactly how many people I spoke to that month. I mark the ones I closed with a green color (the color of money!) to remind myself which ones actually turned into real clients.

This system will give you an easy way to see a few important pieces of information. If you're not getting many leads for your business, that detail will be easily documented in your system. When you know your numbers, you can then create a plan of action to improve your processes or figure out where you can make additional enhancements.

### *Your Turn: Note Taking and Tracking Your Clients*

*Choose your systems for the following:*

> 1.  *Writing notes: Do you want to type them out or write them down by hand?*
>
> 2.  *Keeping track of your clients: Do you want to use a CRM or a simple spreadsheet?*

*Once you decide on particular methods, write them down in your journal. For CRM and tracking systems, ask your other entrepreneurial friends or people in online forums like Facebook groups which systems they like to use and why, in order to help narrow your search.*

*Get into the habit of documenting each of your prospective clients and include in your notes specific information related to their personal lives (like where they live and whether they have kids), their major issues related to their current or past situations, and what their goals are.*

## Day 24: Following Up

Now let's talk about the follow-up process. If someone expresses an interest in your product or service, but they say that they need some time to "get their act together" before moving forward, there could be a few matters occurring. They could be politely trying to decline, but are afraid of actually saying "no" to you. Maybe they had bad experiences in the past with pushy salespeople, who give us a bad name! They are hesitant to be upfront because they think that you will try to push them into taking an action they're not ready for.

Perhaps they still have some concerns either internally or externally. Maybe they don't think that they have enough time for your program. I personally think this idea is often an excuse for people because if something is important to you, then you'll make time for it. The same concept goes for money. If you have a deep pain and you are ready to solve that problem, you will invest what it takes to solve that problem because it's such a glaring need at that moment.

There are legitimate times when the person genuinely needs you to follow up with them. For example, I spoke to a coach about digital marketing services for one of the agencies I do sales for and he was excited to get started. We positioned ourselves as experts and showed him some of our case studies. We also did a great job identifying his pain points and needs.

However, he was still finishing up his coaching certification, and since he had just immigrated to the United

States, he didn't have any credit history to apply for credit cards or get a loan. He literally didn't have any way to pay for our services at that moment. He was, therefore, a great candidate for a follow up.

I try to pinpoint an actual date to follow up with a person and the method that they prefer. Some people will set up a follow-up call with you while others want you to send them an email to check in with them at a certain time. CRM systems are great for these types of scheduling issues because most of them have a function to remind you to either make the call or send out the email message.

If the person does not commit to a certain date for the follow up, then it's up to you to periodically check in with them. This assessment also goes for people who decided to go with another provider. Sometimes you'll luck out and find that the person is not happy with the provider they chose.

Maybe they saw you as an expert in your field, but then in the end went with the other option because it was cheaper. But cheaper doesn't always mean they will save time and money. In fact, if a task is not done right the first time, the prospective client may learn the hard way that they should have just paid your fees upfront instead!

Follow up with the person in the same proportion as your desire for the deal. When you follow up with them, don't just write them an ordinary, "Just wanted to touch base with you" message. Provide some value to them. Give them a blog post that reminded you of them and their specific situation. Ask them whether they have been able to solve the problem related to their individual paint point.

Here's an example of a follow up email which applies to my business:

*Hi Prospective Client,*

*I was thinking of you the other day and was wondering if you were able to solve your issues surrounding your fears on selling yourself. I remember the conversation we had where you shared that you wanted to be able to sell without having that anxious feeling inside. The extra income would help you save up for that dream vacation to Bali.*

*Feel free to reach out if I can be of service to you in any way. I'm happy to hop on another call with you to get some updates on your situation. You can schedule with my online link below.*

*Thanks so much and have a great day!*

*Jula*

*P.S. I wrote this new blog post on how to overcome anxiety when pitching a newly-raised price. Check it out right here (insert link). Let me know what you think of it!*

Create a general email follow up template like the one above and keep it handy in a labeled email folder or some other organized place. That way you can access it anytime you need to. Many CRM's will allow you to create email templates in their systems and then email the client directly from the CRM. You can edit the templates as needed to make them more personal.

### *Your Turn: Write a Follow-Up Email Template*

*Use the above example of a follow-up email to create your own template. Insert a blank space for places where you will personalize the email using the notes that you've taken during the call with your prospective client.*


*Create a folder in your email or an online storage space like Google Drive or Dropbox and put the email template there for quick and easy reference!*

# Day 25: Mindset Routine for Sales

Just as it's important to have rituals surrounding your own mindset routines, it is also a great idea to get into the habit of preparing yourself mentally for sales calls. As you've dug deep to unearth your limiting beliefs about money, as well as your own sales abilities, you've also uncovered your own resilience. You need that resilience to stay strong when people say no, to not take the refusal personally, and to be able to quickly move your focus onto your next prospective client.

When I first started doing sales with a higher price point, I was nervous about my calls. I often felt my heart beating when I began my pitching process and I waited in anxious anticipation for the client to inevitably mention the price or my lack of case studies. This nervous state was not ideal in preparing for my sales calls, but my body couldn't help it.

That's why it's a good idea to figure out ahead of time what you need to do to settle and even inspire your mind before you begin your calls. For example, you might visualize yourself actually taking the calls, connecting with your clients, laughing with them, asking them the right questions, intelligently answering all their objections, and having them provide their credit card numbers, all without you even beginning a call! Visualization is an extremely powerful tool and it only needs a bit of imagination and quiet time to yourself.

You can visualize yourself helping your prospective client. Imagine how happy that person will feel when you provide them your particular service. Will your service allow them to spend less time working? Will they live a healthier, more fulfilled life? Can you see them playing with their kids, spending time with their partners, going on more vacations, all because of you?

I also like to write down these visualizations in my journal. I've read in multiple books that there's a power in using the present tense when you write about a situation, as though you are actually living it in the now. However, recently I read another money mindset book where the author mentioned that it's better to write in the past, as though a situation already happened. I thought that perspective was brilliant! Your mind will believe that the event already occurred and will take the vision at face value.

The main goal before you jump on a sales call is to feel really enthusiastic about it. You want to feel pumped, invigorated, motivated by your mission, charged up, and ready to go. If you're feeling under the weather or have just received bad news and are trying to process it, these issues will most definitely affect your sales calls. It's better if you can reschedule those calls or spend a few minutes resetting your mindset.

One of the ways I really pump myself up before sales calls is listening to inspiring music. One of my sales mentors told me about the song "Glorious," by the rapper Macklemore. Although I don't tend to gravitate towards that type of music, something about the song uplifted me. I felt like I could do anything and that there was so much abundance and hope in the world. That's the type of song that is worth your while to listen to before you start your sales calls.

The other routine which also invigorated me was standing in a power pose. This practice especially worked right before a pitch. I literally stood like Wonder Woman, with my two hands in fists on either side of my waist and my feet planted firmly on the ground, my legs forming an inverted "v" shape. I also put my chest out, standing tall and strong. It is an incredibly powerful position to be in and you really feel as though you can handle anything that comes your way, including unanticipated objections or questions!

Whatever you choose or experiment with - whether it's watching an inspiring video, listening to music, meditating, or visualizing - you can incorporate these motivational tools into your overall sales routine, and these practices will help elevate your sense of confidence on your calls. Find the techniques that make you feel as though you can conquer anything in the world.

Speaking to yourself in this positive way can also make you feel energized and motivated before your calls. When I think back over all the times I was so harsh and critical of myself, pointing out my own flaws, I feel regret. Treat yourself with kindness, the way you would a friend. Remind yourself of your strengths. If you need help, review the list of accomplishments you made in a previous exercise and internally tell yourself that you can do this!

### *Your Turn: Mindset Exercises Before Your Sales Call*

*Prior to one of your sales calls, choose to either listen to one of your favorite empowering songs or stand in a powerful pose. After the call, write in your journal what you noticed. Did you feel as though you had more confidence on your call? Did you assert yourself differently? How will this feeling affect your calls in the future?*

# Week 6

# Day 26: Developing a Resilient Mind

Selling is really what you make of it. If you believe that selling is hard and that people always shop around for the lowest bargain, you're going to manifest that type of customer. If you think that people will ghost you by not responding to your emails and phone calls, they will. Your mind is an incredibly powerful and sensitive tool and it pays to develop it in ways to attract what you want. Stop thinking so long and hard about what you don't want because then you'll get obsessed with bad scenarios and unconsciously manifest them.

Developing a resilient mind means that you don't let certain things bother you on a fundamental level. Or, if you're dealing with a stress in your life, you can more easily bounce back from feeling frazzled. Believe me, I've had my days when I do not want to get on sales calls and all I want to do is ruminate on my issues and feel sorry for myself. But deep down, I knew that my mindset did not help the situation.

You will not close every single person you meet, nor do you want to. You have to keep that fact in mind! You're going to go through different cycles and feelings. Some days I feel really motivated and capable of writing thousands of words. Other days, it's a challenge to squeak past the 1000-word goal I have for myself. You'll feel the same way about selling.

For the days when you feel down and several clients reject or ghost you in a row, you need to find a way to snap yourself out of that state of mind. Negativity just feeds upon itself. You can start to look at your situation differently and reframe it. For example, remind yourself that even though you've heard "no" so many times, it can mean a "yes" is right around the corner. You can also be grateful that someone said no to you because it may have averted a situation where you had to deal with a potentially difficult client.

I used to take no's personally and blamed myself when I wasn't closing a lot of clients. The way I got over this feeling was remembering the times when I did have success and reminding myself that my current situation was a temporary situation. When you have a series of no's, it's often difficult to stay positive and optimistic. Low energy issues can also mess with cash flow issues. Your energy may be subconsciously repelling prospective clients. Your issues may reveal themselves in subtle ways, such as in the tone of your voice.

Your mindset is key to your success, so take good care of it. Don't let negative people deter you from reaching your goals. Learn what you can do better in your sales conversations and then move on. Talk to yourself in a way which is encouraging rather than criticizing or cutting. I learned the technique of being more gentle with myself from therapy. You have to learn how to nurture and be kind to yourself, much like you are kind to a friend who's going through a difficult time.

Having a strong mindset will lead you to achieve your goals. And when you get that sale, the feeling is intoxicating! But don't let that move you off course because there's going to be the next lead or phone call right around the corner. Celebrate your wins, but don't spend too much time gloating about them. You want your highs to be as smooth as your lows. Feel your emotions and then release them.

Also, watch your thoughts throughout the day. If you continually tell yourself that sales is hard and that acquiring new clients is a tough process, then that's what you're going to manifest. If you say over and over to yourself that people are not able to spend that much money on your type of services, then guess what? That's right! You are the creator of the reality. Your thoughts are incredibly powerful, so pay attention to the words in your mind.

Be careful about the words which come forth from you in your everyday conversations as well. Observe the ways in which you complain to people in your life about either how your sales calls went or all the things you did wrong in your calls. Yes, it's important to self-reflect and think about the ways to make your sales calls go more smoothly. However, it won't help you to beat yourself up about situations that happened or to ruminate about other moments that were not even in your control.

Remind yourself that it's not the end of the world when you didn't close a deal that you thought you had in your grasp. There's more to you and to your life than closing one sale. Yes, it can be frustrating in the moment, but it can also be an opportunity for your own growth. Because with each no, you do get stronger. You can find ways to challenge those no's. Remember, you come from a place of serving others and you genuinely want to help them. So, their no is not always in their best interest.

Focus on what you can change and give yourself positive compliments for the things that you did well. For example, maybe you didn't close a new prospective client who seemed like the perfect fit for you on the surface. However, you can be proud of yourself for the level of rapport and connection you developed with that person.

When all else fails, take a break from your sales efforts and be gentle with yourself. One day, I had a series of no's that were extremely disheartening and frustrating. I ended up going to my partner and asking him for a hug because I needed a pick-me-up. I did feel better! The hug also reminded me of what was important in my life.

Taking a break is the perfect time to regroup and reassess where you are. You can shift out of a negative mindset by either taking a break, going for a walk, talking with a friend about non-business-related matters, or exercising. Do something which makes you feel rejuvenated and give yourself a break from that sense of pressure. You'll be able to develop a more resilient mind when you're feeling refreshed and capable of tackling a new situation.

Finally, laughter can also be a beneficial remedy when you're feeling down about not getting a deal. I sometimes watch funny movies or videos to cheer me up and this hiatus also helps me clear my mind to bring more joy. Laughter helps me not take myself so seriously and gives me an opportunity to find the positives again in my situation.

I think it's important to feel what you are feeling, but it's dangerous to ruminate in those emotions and to start to go down the path of thinking that you're not good enough.

## Your Turn: Affirmations for Developing a Resilient Mind

*In your journal, write out at least three affirmations that you can say to yourself throughout the day in order to cultivate a resilient mind. Here are a few examples:*

1. *I am an expert at what I do and my prospective clients recognize this.*
2. *I close prospective clients easily and effectively.*
3. *Clients are excited to work with me and happily pay for my services.*
4. *My business is growing in leaps and bounds effortlessly.*

*Practice these affirmations out loud and say them with feeling. Revisit them when you are having a bad day or need a quick pick me up.*

*If you experience a series of rejections or no's during your sales process, take a break and treat yourself to something special like lunch with a friend or a walk. Press the restart button and rejuvenate your mind!*

# Day 27: Handling Ghosted Clients

I have to admit that one of my biggest pet peeves in being a salesperson is dealing with ghosted clients. If you're not familiar with the term, ghosting is when a person seemed quite interested in your services originally and you had many back-and-forth conversations. Then all of a sudden, they seem to disappear into thin air. You attempt to contact them several times with the typical, "Hey, just wanted to check in" email. You leave messages on their phone. But there's absolutely no response. It's as if they never existed.

Ghosting is incredibly annoying, but it doesn't have to throw off your mindset!

I have several theories about why people ghost. Some prospective clients are just negligent about getting back in touch because they are so overwhelmed with their own lives and businesses. Others are afraid of telling someone no to his face because they think that salesperson will try to convince them otherwise. Or perhaps they had bad experiences in the past. Saying no can be an uncomfortable task if you're used to saying yes, all the time.

Then, there are the prospective clients who find another bargain or potential provider with whom they connected and they feel uncomfortable about telling you. Still others are not ready to commit themselves or the money but they couldn't admit that out loud, so instead they disappear. Maybe there's a hint of embarrassment or shame that they carry around.

When I worked for an agency in the UK, I interacted with clients from all over the world - Sweden, India, New Zealand, and England. I found that the US had higher numbers of ghosted clients. Perhaps ghosting is also a cultural standard. Many people are often distracted by their emails and notifications, while others shop around for the lowest deal or the "best" provider in their eyes. They do lots of different interviews but they don't feel an obligation to inform the other salespeople of their choice.

The other possibility for being ghosted is that your sales call did not convince them that they needed your services and they did not feel a social obligation to give you feedback about it. In this case, you can review your recorded call and see if there was something in particular which you could have said and done differently. Were you being a bit too aggressive in trying to get a deposit? Was it your tone of voice? Did you come off as being desperate on the call?

Ghosting happens to the best of us. I've closed hundreds of thousands in new business and I deal with disappearing prospective clients on a regular basis. The trick to dealing with ghosting is to not take it personally and to just move onto the next prospective client. It's good to analyze your own call and see what you could have done differently, but there's also a high likelihood that the disappearance is more about them than you.

If you think that there's an area you can improve about your sales process, get feedback from someone you trust or bounce ideas off your coach, if you have one. Listen to podcasts, read blogs about sales, and strive to improve every single day. Check your mindset. Did you unconsciously put off the prospective client because you are anxious about money and they sensed that insecurity?

Don't agonize over what you "should" have done. My biggest advice for working with ghosted clients is to just brush it off. Your mental energy is too precious and there are plenty of fish in the sea. The ghosted client was probably someone you wouldn't want to interact with as a regular client anyway because ghosting is not an ideal form of communication! You would probably have a lot of difficulties trying to work with them in the long run.

That being said, sometimes you may feel that you need some closure for the situation. If you would like to get a reaction out of your ghosted client, here's an email template which I use to attempt to get them to respond to me:

*Hi Prospective Client,*

*Hope you're doing well.*

*I didn't hear back from you in regards to my voicemail and email messages, so I just wanted to check in.*

*Typically, when I don't hear back from prospective clients, it could be one of three reasons:*

> *1. They are extremely busy and haven't had the time to answer my messages.*

> *2. They are no longer interested in our services and/or have chosen to work with another vendor.*

> *3. They still have some concerns and questions about the proposal or our company in general.*

*I would appreciate you taking the time to write me a short message and explain which of the scenarios apply to you.*

*Thanks again for your response and have a wonderful day!*

*Jula*


I have received several responses to the above email and a lot of the time, people are just genuinely busy. I found that the email gives people the benefit of the doubt and it helps alleviate some of the frustration on your end. I also find that sending out this email gives me a personal sense of closure, whether or not I actually get a response from them. I know that I can be proud of myself for doing my best in following up with the client and putting out the effort.

If someone has decided to go with another provider and they decided not to tell you, that's okay. If you thought they were a potentially good client for you, you still have the option of following up with them on an occasional basis and asking how their business is doing. You may discover that they are not happy with the company that they chose and are actually looking for another provider.


### *Your Turn: Handling Ghosted Clients*

A. *When someone has ghosted you, visualize the client in front of you and imagine yourself thanking them for their time. Now visualize them exiting a door. On the other side of the door, there's a queue of new clients waiting to speak to you. Let the next one in.*

**B.** *Use the above template to create your own email to send out to ghosted clients. You are welcome to use mine word for word or you can inject your own personality into it. Save it in your cloud, your CRM, or a labeled email folder so that you have easy access to it.*

# Day 28: Internet Marketing Gurus

You've come so far with your mindset and your sales process. I commend you for the hard work you've done! I am a big believer in celebrating big and small wins, and you're at a point where you can pat yourself on the back and do something fun to acknowledge where you are at in your journey. It takes a lot of discipline to get through this process.

As your six-week challenge draws closer to the end, I want to take a moment to talk about something which I am extremely passionate about. One of the main reasons that I get fired up about this topic is that I spent ten years of my life believing the words of a manipulator who happened to be a charismatic leader.

Because I was taken advantage of in my own life, I am particularly sensitive to the fact that many people are taken advantage of on a daily basis, just like I once was. Unfortunately, there are unethical people who are more concerned with power and money than actually helping others.

You've probably seen the ads for internet marketing gurus who claim that you can grow your business if you just drop $10,000 or more on their online programs. They often plaster pictures of themselves standing in front of their personal jets or Lamborghinis, suggesting that you too can have the freedom and lifestyle of your dreams if you just follow them.

As a business owner, you have to be careful of deceptive people who claim to know the true path. We are inundated all the time with images and advertisements on the internet which promise us certain experiences. There are people who take advantage of those are looking for legitimate qualities in their lives - more time with their families, financial freedom, and growth for their businesses. But not all coaches are made equal.

My advice is for you to become a critical thinker when you evaluate internet coaches and programs. When clients choose to work with me, I even encourage them to do their research on my business programs. Whether you want to learn how to improve your branding, build your business up, or learn more sales techniques, always critically examine the person who offers the program or one-on-one coaching.

When you evaluate whether or not a program or coach is legitimate and the right fit for you, there are several important factors that you need to check:

## 1. Don't get caught up in the hype.

It's easy to get pulled into the fantasy of flying to Thailand and working from there while sipping on some elaborate tropical mixed drink, but this dream is out of reach for most people that buy into outrageous internet programs. Don't get pulled into the hype that internet marketing gurus try to create. If they make outrageous promises or pull on your heart strings, step back and see how they have you envision your own goals by creating a fantastical, but unrealistic "dreamscape."

Some of these coaches have good intentions in mind and really want to help you. However, there are many people who try to emotionally connect with you because they are more interested in your money than genuinely helping you.

## 2. Read through their testimonials and case studies carefully.

Many of these gurus will try to leverage their social proof to show how great their programs are. Oftentimes, it's good to take these testimonials with a grain of salt because they only show you students that are the cream of the crop. You'll probably read several disclaimers on the bottom of their landing pages which state that certain results are not common. When you read through testimonials and case studies, keep this in mind and read the fine print!

When in doubt, it's best to talk to several people from the group who've actually gone through the course before. Try to verify the results of the case studies and determine if the information you see is actually true or not by contacting the participants directly, if they have given their names. And of course, keep in mind that the coaches will not share their tough situations!

## 3. Talk to someone who has used the program and ask them to tell you one strength of the program as well as one weakness.

When I was about to sign up for my $10k program, I reached out to as many people as I could to try to have an actual conversation with someone who went through it. This conversation can be a bit tricky because most of the people who actually will speak to you about the program are already superfans, and they will only have good things to say about the coach.

Finding someone who has a balanced perspective of the program and is able to give you more unbiased feedback is more difficult to do. I once asked a person to tell me the strengths and weaknesses of a certain teacher for a sales program and he only described to me about the positives of the teacher. When I pressed him for a negative feature, he had nothing to say.

Another former graduate from that same program said the only negative thing was being around some people who weren't as motivated as others. But this statement was not a direct criticism of the teacher or the program itself!

Be wary of people who have nothing negative to say because they've either been brainwashed to be extra-positive or they are afraid of saying anything critical to deter you from entering the program. I prefer when people are honest and upfront about a program or teacher's drawbacks, because let's face it, everyone has their weaknesses. Those people who are self-aware and honest will tell you where the weaknesses lie.

### 4. Google the coach and read as many articles and reviews as you can about him or her.

Do your research on the business coach and see if any specific complaints come up about him or her. This investigation also includes reading all the positive and negative reviews about the person or organization. You may dredge up some interesting information! I've spent a lot of time reading through articles which the coaches have written online to see how legitimate they are in their particular area of expertise. Check their credentials, where they studied, as well as the reputations of their colleagues and team members.

**5. Pay attention to their sales process and how it makes you feel.**

The sales process itself will tell you a lot about how a particular coach functions. As you can tell by now, I'm not a big fan of slimy sales tactics which are designed to get you to feel a certain way or push you into joining just for the sake of money. Did you feel supported during the sales process or did you feel like they simply wanted you to act on their offer? Did they use false scarcity tactics or limited time offers to persuade you? How did that approach feel to you?

If you sense you were pushed into a certain direction or that your emotions were triggered just to get the sale out of you, pay attention to those feelings. It may be time to take a step back and reevaluate if this company is the best choice for you. It's quite possible the program is more interested in your money rather than you as a person.

**6. Ask the right questions.**

Be direct with your questions and ask about the successes and failures of students or clients that the coach has worked with before. Have them describe their programs to you and how they were created. What was the background of the head coach or teacher and how did they get to achieve their success? Be curious and cover your bases. Ask also about the roles of different staff members and who you would work with directly.

## 7. Trust your gut and use your common sense.

At the end of the day, you have to trust your gut on whether or not an expensive program is right for you. There's an element of trust required because you won't know exactly what you're getting into until you are in the program. Be cautious in your decision and use your common sense. If something doesn't feel right, take note of this. For example, if the program feels cult-like by the type of language the group uses or the group members cannot say anything bad about the leader, you should find another program.

You are an educated person and you have the power to make good decisions.

### *Your Turn: Evaluating a Coach or Program*

*If you are in the midst of evaluating a coach or certain online program, read through several testimonials and write down some of the outcomes that the program suggests or promises. Try to find at least one person who has graduated from that program and ask them about their specific experiences. Be sure to ask them about the positives and negatives of the program and pay close attention to their answer about the negatives. If it seems too good to be true, then the program probably is.*

# Day 29: Determine What You Want

I think most women get caught up in the hype of online gurus because of one fundamental reason - we have a hard time trusting ourselves. I'm sure that there are a lot of women who grew up feeling as though they could take on the world and had the support from role models to be confident in themselves. But I didn't grow up feeling that way. I relied on other people to reflect my worth back to me. And this lack of confidence put me in a spot where I was vulnerable to outside influences.

You are the creator of your life and your business. You are perfectly capable of getting clear on what you want and how you want to manifest it. Many of those big online gurus use certain marketing techniques to play on your emotions because they know that's what's going to get you to part ways with your cash.

You've heard those stories about how some people started out living on their relatives' couches, but all of a sudden, they found a "secret" formula, read a few books, or turned to their mentors in order to find the key to making their first million. And now, they supposedly have all this freedom, fly all over the world, and buy whatever they want.

That might be someone's idea of paradise, but it's not exactly my dream! In those stories of becoming an internet millionaire and finding freedom, I don't detect the ways those people want to help humanity or make an impact on this planet. Yes, some of them start foundations and donate to charities but their focus seems only to be on making money. I believe that money makes you more of who you already are. Money is not the root of evil - evil people are.

But because we have so many decisions to make in our lives, it feels easier to just rely upon other people to tell you what you want for your business. Sometimes we simply go with what they say is right for us.

That absence of knowing what I wanted for my life is exactly how I got caught up in the supposed dream of making $100k per month for my digital marketing agency with a team of eight people underneath me. I bought into a program and felt pressured to build my business up in a certain way. I didn't realize that I wanted a different path for myself.

Working to make myself fit into someone else's dream only resulted in a lot of stress and heartache. I didn't take advantage of the gifts and talents that were innately mine. I kept trying to be someone I wasn't.

Give yourself permission to make your business what you want it to be, and don't fall into the trap of listening to those online gurus. You are your own person with your own unique set of gifts, talents, and dreams, and no one can take that away from you. If you want to be a stay-at-home mother and work only a few hours per week, then that's your priority. If you want to start an ecommerce business selling herbal soaps and gross $1 million or more per year, then go for it!

You need the time and space to think about what you truly want. And some coaches and teachers can get you there through their caring guidance. But they are not your be-all, end-all. You are the mover and shaker of your own life and you need to learn to love yourself enough and believe yourself enough in order to make your business work for you.

I wish when I was young that I had more role models reinforce this confidence in my life. When I was younger, I had such a low sense of self-esteem that I didn't really believe other people when they said I had potential. For example, I always wanted to be a writer and I often got commended for my writing skills in school, from my sixth grade English teacher to my creative writing teacher in college. However, for a very long time, I didn't believe in myself enough to pursue writing.

Think first about what your ultimate goals are; then you can work backwards to find out how many leads to generate and sales to close in order to make that dream happen. Dig deep within yourself and ask what will make you profitable, balanced, and happy, while using your unique gifts and talents to help the world be a better place.

You already have what you need. It's inside you.

### *Your Turn: Determining What You Want in the Perfect Day*

*Write down the vision for your perfect day in your business and life by answering these questions:*

1. *What are you doing when you wake up?*
2. *What are you eating for breakfast?*
3. *Are you exercising or doing a yoga class?*
4. *Are you meditating or writing in your journal?*

5. *How many hours per day are you working?*

6. *What are your work hours during the day?*

7. *How many clients per week are you working with?*

8. *How do your clients feel after working with you?*

9. *How much are you earning per day?*

10. *What are you doing in the evenings?*

11. *How much time are you spending with your partner, kids, family, or friends each day?*

12. *When are you going to sleep?*


*Visualization is a powerful tool for helping you tap into what you want and begin to manifest it in everyday life!*

# Day 30: To Scale or Not to Scale

As you get better and better at sales, you'll see your company taking off. Your demand may increase and you'll experience some growing pains. You'll have to make a decision on whether you want to keep the company small or begin to scale it. That choice all goes back to the question of what you want and what you feel is right for you and your business.

Not everyone needs to scale their business to a $10 million company. Not everyone has the time, desire, or resources to make that investment. It takes a lot of grit and determination, as well as a keen ability to hire and train the right people for the right roles. Some people thrive on expansion, but that growth might not be right for you.

I genuinely thought I wanted a business which would help me achieve big revenue goals. I thought I could build a team beneath me. I didn't stop to think about whether this direction was a dream I had just because so many people on the internet wanted it or if that vision truly came from inside me.

You can structure the life and the business you want to fit into what is important to you. Right now, having a business that makes multi-millions is not my priority. My priority is my partner, my family, my friends, my health, writing, and my hobbies such as playing the ukulele and taking voice lessons.

I don't have the type of ambition some people possess and that's perfectly okay. I am content with having two assistants in my business and me. Yes, it would be great to eventually make $30k per month or more including some passive income, but I am not willing to compromise my happiness and my relationships in order to do that.

My desires and dreams may change in the future. I have a vision to attract more and more women to my cause because I feel deeply compelled to give them tools and knowledge to empower their lives and businesses. I love teaching and coaching because I see so many women struggling with the exact same things that I went through, and it's gratifying to be able to help them see the light at the other end of the tunnel.

Fulfilling my purpose is more important to me than just having a huge company for the sake of earning more money or being admired by other people. I want to know that I'm making a deep impact on this planet. The main reason I might want to scale up my business is the thought that I could help more women and impact even more lives. That dream is my why and what truly drives me.

However, I also realize that as we work through our own issues around success, you don't want to limit your thinking about what is possible. So, it pays to ask yourself - are you afraid of your own success? Do you have a history of sabotaging your circumstances when they are going well? Have you created your own glass ceiling because you want to keep life a certain way?

As entrepreneurs, we will experience fear and discomfort during our growth phase. It's so essential to do your daily mindset practice and get more clear about what you want to help combat those feelings of fear. You have many tools to be able to manifest your goals bit by bit. And you will meet the right people to help you. Perhaps you won't always make the right decisions in that moment in time, but you'll learn from every experience.

I can't say I'm 100% proud of every decision that I made because some of them led to conflicts with other people, financial debt, and discomfort. But I learned from all of my mistakes and processed through them so that I could take that knowledge for the next time I face a major decision.

The most important advice I want to impart is that you don't have to listen to or follow someone else when it comes to determining whether or not you want to scale. Your business is your own and scaling is a very personal decision. Just because you see someone else doing it, doesn't mean you automatically have to follow their lead. Be confident in your own vision! Follow your own intuition on what's right for you.

### *Your Turn: How Big Do You Want to Scale?*

*Write in your journal your ultimate vision for your company and how much money you want to make for your business. Do you want a small team or a big one? Do you want to stay a freelancer? What do you think will bring your ultimate happiness?*

# Learning to Trust Yourself

When I first lost my job in 2015, and decided to launch into the world of entrepreneurship, I had many uneasy feelings. I had so many new skills to learn or to revisit, including social media marketing, Facebook ads, funnels, marketing myself, keeping track of my payments with an invoicing system, hiring contractors, firing contractors, and doing sales for my company. This mass of information to grasp definitely felt overwhelming at times, but also deeply satisfying. Your business is like your child and it is a joy to watch it flourish and grow. Something creative comes from a vision that is so personal and it's you. Such inspiration comes from your core essence.

As I began my new business, I made tons of mistakes, some of which I'm not too proud of. I hired people I *should* not have. I often underpriced myself when I *should* have asked for more. I got into a lot of credit card debt because I convinced myself I *should* keep putting in more effort. The word that stands out the most to me in each of those previous sentences is "should." We think we *should* be doing something differently.

The truth is that entrepreneurship will grow you and stretch you in unimaginable ways. You'll feel a high one day and an extreme low another day. Some days you'll soar, enjoying the freedom to have a cup of coffee with your best girlfriend whenever you want. Other days you'll dream of having a stable paycheck again. Owning your own business can be a rollercoaster ride.

I'm always amazed at how many incredible women I meet every single day -- whether it's in my personal life, my coaching practice, or my business -- who struggle with the same fundamental issues. Our culture ingrained in us from an early age that we are not enough. We are told that money, looks, and status make us whole rather than that our worth is tied to external values. It often feels like we worked hard to chase a dream that wasn't even ours to begin with. We don't value what we have to offer the world.

I want to tell you that it's okay to be just you! It's okay to be creative, take risks, make mistakes, mess up on your sales calls, and make statements that you *shouldn't* have. You gain knowledge every single step of the way and you can be proud of the person that you are growing into, the woman you are becoming.

I joined an expensive online program because fundamentally I wanted to learn to do one thing -- trust myself. I wanted to prove to myself and the world that I was good enough. But the recognition that we are "enough" cannot be seen externally. There's an internal experience and transformation that is extremely personal. And this realization doesn't have anything to do with how many clients you have, how many speaking events you've attended, or how much money you make in your business. You just make the decision that you are enough.

It's easy to get caught up under the spells of online marketing gurus or even start to compare yourself to other women entrepreneurs in your industry because from the outside, it seems alluring to have external success alone. But that's why I go back to my own mindset routine; I feel grounded in my daily acts of gratitude and my commitment to my body and my health. No one can take that mindset away from me and no one can knock me off my center.

When I am steady in my mind, I am more confident in my abilities. My confidence will prevent me from being taken in by schemes or comparing myself to others.

Learning to trust yourself means that you have the confidence to learn skills which take you out of your comfort zone. Perhaps doing sales isn't something which comes naturally to you, but it is a learnable skill. Perhaps you grew up in an environment which did not support your dreams, so you began to believe that you couldn't accomplish what you wanted. But you can change that limited mindset. You're not a slave to your past and you dictate your future.

I have a vision for more and more women to awaken to their inner power and claim who they already are. I went through a very painful process in order to realize that I was actually valuable inside. I had to nurture the little girl inside me who didn't get the type of love and attention she needed at certain points of her life. I've been deceived and mistreated before. But that's not my identity.

Stay true to your personal mission and uncover the passion inside you which is already waiting to come out. You have a special message to bring to your clients and students. You are a changemaker and you can make a difference with your own personal, unique talents. You don't have to convince every single person around you. The most important person to convince is yourself.

So, trust yourself. Trust that you can find the power to fulfill your dream of having a thriving a business. Eradicate those critical voices and the thoughts inside yourself that constantly pick apart everything that you do or say. Silence all of them and listen to your soul. You have the capacity to build a business which nurtures you, financially sustains you, and brings you joy. You don't have to be a slave to your business. Your vision can liberate you.

I've come from many situations where I didn't feel empowered. It's part of my journey. But I don't think that I would be able to teach women now if I hadn't gone through that pain and suffering. I have gained empathy for people who feel stuck with their financial glass ceilings, who struggle with their self-worth and who lack the confidence to bring out their own voice. I once was there too.

I am really grateful for all the experiences I have gone through because they made me the person I am today. They were all part of my own personal journey. I did the best I could with what I knew and what I had. Your journey is also what makes you the person you are today. Keep your wins list handy and refer to it often. If you can shift your mindset when you're feeling stressed and lethargic, you can have the power to bring out more positive emotions.

I believe it's the birthright of every woman on this planet to feel secure in herself, confident, and empowered. She can live a life of abundance and prosperity without having to justify herself. My hope is that you will take the simple principles I discussed throughout this book and apply them to your own life. Treat yourself with kindness and gentleness. Remember to speak encouragement to yourself.

You're going to stumble. You're going to make mistakes. You're going to have bad days. That's okay. But what's more important is to put one foot in front of the other, learn to forgive yourself, and take the effort to make small changes which will impact bigger areas in your life and your business. I have worked hard on letting go of the past and celebrating my progress and I encourage my clients to cherish their own journeys as well.

If you need help along the way, there are many people and resources out there to support you. Be sure to do your homework researching them and seeking out recommendations! If you feel motivated to work with me through either one-on-one coaching or through one of my group coaching programs, you can find more information through my website at www.ontimesocial.com or you can schedule a time to chat with me personally at www.calendly.com/julapereira.

I would also be honored to hear from you directly about the biggest takeaway you got from this book. I read all my email personally and will send you a message back. It may take me a few days to respond, but I definitely will. I enjoy hearing the stories of brave women who've decided to make a big change in their lives and face their fears head on. That's what is so satisfying in my work - seeing other people grow and thrive. So, feel free to email me at jula@julapereira.com.

It's been a wonderful journey together. Here's to your success and abundance!

# Acknowledgements

Many people impacted my life and made me the person I am today. If I haven't listed your name specifically, know that I deeply appreciate all your support and friendship. You know who you are.

First and foremost, thank you to all my English and Literature teachers who believed in my writing talent from the start.

I am deeply grateful to all my mentors and supervisors who gave me excellent advice on life and business.

To the powerful women influencers who have inspired me to no end.

To my closest friends, business colleagues, and confidantes who cheered me on along the way and made me laugh when I needed it the most.

To all my social media marketing clients who trusted me with increasing their visibility and elevating their brands.

To all the amazing sales coaching clients and students with whom I've had the privilege of working, especially my beta students of Six Weeks to Sales Confidence.

Thank you to my self-care and advocate team.

Special thanks to Andrea McCurry for her amazing editing skills which brought this book to life.

To Heidi Margocsy and Tara Baxter from In Her Image Photography for my branding photo shoot and Elise Bigley for my natural make-up look for the photos.

To Michael Corwin for his fantastic book cover design.

Thank you for all the love and support of my family: Les Pereira, Freda Pereira, Laila Pereira, and Michael Pereira.

You've seen me through so much. And Ayaka Osakabe, thank you for taking good care of my brother.

Finally, to my biggest supporter of all and my rock, my partner Joerg Hilger. You've inspired me to be the best person I can be by pushing me beyond my comfort zone and helping me believe in myself. I am so grateful for your love, laughter, and support.

## About the Author

Jula Pereira is a sales professional who mentors women to have more confidence on sales calls. She has closed hundreds of thousands of dollars in new business and has experience speaking at events.

In her free time, she enjoys reading, baking, and hanging out at the beach in beautiful Northern California with her partner and their dog Timmy.

Made in the USA
Las Vegas, NV
25 June 2021